To Clare
from your lifetime
friend
Jeanne

And best wishes
from
Tony Henderson

My Country

Discovering North East England

Volume II

Written and compiled by

Tony Henderson

To my wife Gillian who has matched me step for step.

Our grateful thanks to the following for the images used in this book:
Barry Pells, Jayne Emsley, Tim McGuinness, Ian Winter, Paul Norris,
Simon Hobson, Simon Greener, Matt Offer.

All contact details, prices and site details are correct at time of publication.

First published in 2006 by: At Heart Limited, 32 Stamford Street,
Altrincham, Cheshire, WA14 1EY in conjunction with The Journal,
Thomson House, Groat Market, Newcastle NE1 1ED.

ISBN: 1-84547-110-5

Cover picture:
Shillmoor in Upper Coquetdale, Northumberland,
by Tim McGuinness.

Contents

Foreword

Tony Henderson's forerunner to this book explored 33 destinations in the region and opened many people's eyes to our wonderful, diverse landscape and heritage. With sales all over the world, it has encouraged the author to produce another fascinating book, describing many more places of interest.

This new book underlines just how much the region can offer to visitors and locals alike, with stories that bring each subject to life in an interesting and readable manner.

There is so much to do, see and learn in this historic and beautiful region and this exploration of what is there can only boost our increasingly important tourism industry and our sense of pride in the area.

Duke of Northumberland

Introduction

Volume One of *My Country: Discovering North-East England* explored more than 30 special places in this most surprising of regions.

This second instalment doubles that number and is an indication of just how much there is to uncover and enjoy in the North-East's unspoilt and diverse landscapes, overlain with history and each with their own tales to tell.

The deeper one delves, the more there is to find – and the well is far from dry.

The first book visited many of what could be called the region's big set-piece attractions.

This follow-up volume looks at a number of gems which may not have the same high profile, but which are no less important or intriguing for that.

In some cases, the stories of the people behind the places are so compelling that space has been devoted to them, too.

At the time of writing, the North-East is well on the way to winning its third world heritage site.

The Government is to nominate the twin monastery site of Wearmouth-Jarrow as its sole candidate for world status in 2009.

This great monastic centre was the home of the Venerable Bede, one of Europe's greatest scholars, and, in fact, Bede's World in Jarrow features in this book.

Wearmouth-Jarrow would join Hadrian's Wall and Durham Cathedral and Castle in the region in qualifying for this loftiest of designations.

Heritage experts say that it is difficult to think of any other region anywhere which has three world heritage sites in such close proximity.

It is yet more confirmation of the quality of captivating attractions which the North-East has to offer and which now provide us with another round of destinations to appreciate.

Tony Henderson, 2006

Dilston Castle and Chapel

Perched high above the River Tyne tributary called the Devil's Water, there stands testament to one of the most dramatic and tragic episodes in North-East history.

The ruins of Dilston Castle, and the adjacent early 17th Century Catholic chapel, make a romantic grouping overlooking the waterway near Corbridge.

Joined to the chapel by a short stretch of wall is a Jacobean archway. Today, it leads nowhere. Once it was the gateway to a different world.

This was the entrance to the courtyard of Dilston Hall, the palatial mansion

Dilston Chapel

The combination of the sense of great events at Dilston and its setting amid giant redwood trees can capture the visitor.

Just ask Frances Dickinson and Mary Rose Ridley.

Frances fell for Dilston in 1966 at the age of 22, when her family moved to Hexham.

"My father was a great walker and explorer of the countryside and he took me to visit Dilston," says Frances, who now lives in Newcastle.

The 19th Century hall at Dilston had closed as a maternity hospital and the place was boarded up.

Frances says: "It was one of those wonderful summer's evenings with long shadows. The site was deserted and the grass grew high against the castle, which was such a stunning ruin."

Around the same time Frances's mother gave her a novel, Devil Water by the American writer Anya Seton, which was based on the experiences of the

Radcliffes and their fateful involvement in the Jacobite movement.

Frances says: "I became intrigued and absorbed by the whole story. I couldn't understand how this place, which had this wonderful history, was so neglected."

She ended up writing a booklet called The Castle on Devil's Water.

Marriage and a family intervened. Then in 1992 she took a friend to see the Dilston site.

"I thought, 'here I am after all these years and this tremendous ruin is still crumbling and nobody has done anything about it'." So she decided she would, and updated her booklet.

"I had this compelling feeling that this place had to be respected and restored, and take its place in Northumbrian history."

The charity Mencap, which supports people with learning

disabilities, now operated its college from the 19th Century hall and joined Frances in staging a public exhibition at Dilston over two weekends.

"We had an amazing response. Local people turned up with bits and pieces of Jacobite stories," says Frances, who formed an alliance with people like Mary Rose Ridley and retired chief planner John Lodge, from Corbridge.

A grant was won from English Heritage to stabilise the castle and restore the chapel. In 1997 the North Pennines Heritage Trust came on board and took out a 99-year lease on the castle and chapel from Mencap.

Frances and Mary Rose now run the historic Dilston site. Frances has now written two books on the 3rd Earl – The Reluctant Rebel and Tracking a Legend.

Future hopes include the restoration of the 1620 Lord's Bridge spanning Devil's Water which will hopefully include a public access agreement with Allendale Estates.

Frances and Mary Rose have also gathered together Jacobite and Radcliffe relics with the dream of opening a Jacobite centre at Dilston.

Mary Rose, who was born in Corbridge and lives at Mickley Moor West Farm near Stocksfield, remembers playing at Dilston as a youngster. Her friend's father farmed at Dilston Haugh and told stories about the place.

She says: "I've been obsessed by Dilston since I was a child. There was something about Dilston which drew me. The place has a fascinating history and I've always said Dilston picks the people it wants to become involved. "

Dilston Castle

fashioned by James Radcliffe, 3rd Earl of Derwentwater in the early 18th Century.

But, just over 50 years later, this magnificent mansion was swept away, leaving the castle - a fortified tower house built around 1417 - as a stark survivor.

The 3rd Earl, like his hall, did not survive. He was executed, aged 26, in February 1716 on Tower Hill in London.

James Radcliffe, and what should have been a happy life with his young family, fell victim to the turbulent politics of the times, which produced the Jacobite

risings in 1715 and 1745 - a movement which was eventually blown away on the battlefield at Culloden.

It had all started when the Catholic James II - brother of Charles II - fled to France in 1688 and was replaced on the throne by the Protestant William of Orange and his wife Mary.

The supporters of the thus-

In the 19th Century, Dilston attracted another colourful visitor.

Dilston historian Frances Dickinson's research unearthed the story of a woman calling herself Lady Amelia Tudor, who turned up at Dilston in 1866, claiming to be the grand-daughter of John Radcliffe, 4th Earl of Derwentwater.

She claimed to be the rightful Countess of Derwentwater and set up home inside Dilston Castle, with a tarpaulin for a roof.

After she was evicted, she spent 35 days camped on the side of the road at Dilston.

She continued her campaign for several years, was eventually declared bankrupt and her picture collection and what she said were Radcliffe heirlooms were sold by auction in Newcastle. A portrait of James Stuart made £1,000. Amelia died in Shotley Bridge in 1880.

Bridge over Devil's Water

exiled Stuarts were called Jacobites, from *Jacobus*, the Latin for James.

The Stuarts set up a court outside Paris. At the start of the 18th Century, the most prominent Jacobite family in the North-East was the Radcliffes. They had developed close links to the Stuarts, which were to prove disastrous to the 3rd Earl and the family in general.

James's father, Edward Radcliffe, had married into the Stuarts in 1688, by taking as his wife Lady Mary Tudor, daughter of Charles II and his mistress, the actress Moll Davis.

The arranged marriage – the bride was 14 and her husband around 20 years older – did not last. But it did produce four children, one of whom, James Radcliffe, was sent at the age of 13 to the Stuart court in France as a companion for his cousin Prince James, upon whom the hopes of the 1715 rebellion were to centre.

In 1710 James Radcliffe, who was by then aged 20 and had inherited the Derwentwater estates, left France to visit his lands in what is now Cumbria, and in Dilston, where a Jacobean extension had been built onto the 15th Century tower house. James resolved to build his new mansion around the existing structures.

In 1712 James married Catholic heiress Anna Maria Webb, and their son John was born a year later. A new home, wife and child, and landed estates. The future seemed set fair – but history intervened.

In 1714 Queen Anne, sister of Mary, died childless and her Protestant relative, the German-speaking George, Elector of Hanover, was placed on the throne.

The rebellions of 1715 and 1745 sought to overturn the Hanoverian regime and restore the Stuarts.

It was to cost the lives of James Radcliffe and his

A Roman tombstone can be seen in one of Dilston Chapel's walls

Dilston into the melting pot. It had already experienced its ups and downs. There is believed to have been a castle on the site from the 13th Century.

The tower house which remains today was built by Roger Claxton, Lord of Claxton and Horden in County Durham, and was equipped with gun loops, a rare feature for the North but one which denoted status.

Dilston passed by marriage to the Radcliffes, and the chapel replaced an earlier building dedicated to St Mary Magdalene.

The chapel and the Lord's Bridge across the Devil's Water - which became part of the waterside gardens of Dilston Hall - were said to have been financed from money raised for the Gunpowder Plot. Guy Fawkes was said to have been a visitor.

Sir Edward Radcliffe, who fought for Charles I in the Civil War, lost his estates and retired to one of his residences on Lord's Island on Derwentwater in the Lake District.

After the death of the 3rd Earl's son, John, in 1731, Dilston Hall fell into neglect and was occupied by up to 18 families before its eventual demolition.

The present 19th Century Hall was built for Sir John Grey, receiver for the

brother, Charles.

The cause had already accounted for another prominent Northumbrian. Sir John Fenwick, of Wallington, was executed on Tower Hill in 1697, having been accused of high treason.

The historical twist was that Sir John's horse, White Sorrel, which was forfeit to the Crown, stumbled on a molehill while being ridden by King William. The fall killed the monarch, which led to the Jacobite toast to the "little gentleman in black velvet".

The failure of the 1715 rising threw the future of

Devil's Water at Dilston

Derwentwater Estates, and became a maternity home until 1965. It is now used as a college by the charity Mencap.

But the castle, chapel and picturesque Lord's Bridge still speak of the tragic Radcliffes.

The chapel also acts as a memorial to another figure from history. Set into the chapel's external wall is a Roman gravestone featuring the figure of a woman. She may have been buried alongside the nearby Roman road of Dere Street, and is as much a part of the history of Dilston as the Jacobites.

Dilston Castle and chapel are open from late April until the end of September on afternoons from 1pm-4pm, except Saturdays and Mondays.

The Castle Café at the college is open for light refreshments.

Out of season, visitors are asked to call at the café to report their visit and they will usually be able to pick up the keys to the chapel and castle.

Telephone (01434) 382037.

Dilston is off the B6321/A695 roads between Corbridge and Hexham.

Follow the signs to Dilston College.

Jacobite Northumberland

For a tumultuous two weeks in October 1715, rebel forces roamed across Northumberland.

Frances Dickinson in the surviving doorway of the Three Half Moons Inn at Rothbury

The Catholic peer James Radcliffe found himself in this excruciating position mainly because he happened to be cousin to Prince James Francis Edward Stuart.

The 1715 Jacobite rebellion sought to restore the exiled Stuarts to the throne they had vacated when James II fled to France, and to oust the Protestant Hanoverian George.

James Radcliffe, who had no doubt been contemplating a long and prosperous life as a Northumbrian aristocrat, was one of the county's leading Jacobite figures and felt compelled to join the rising.

The movements of the rebel force as it criss-crossed the county, gathering recruits as it waited for an expected French landing of troops and arms, have been painstakingly plotted by Frances Dickinson, as the latest project in her 30-year fascination with the Radcliffes and the castle and chapel they left behind at Dilston.

Frances has produced a Jacobite trail across

One can only guess at the innermost feelings of the man at their head, James Radcliffe, 3rd Earl of Derwentwater.

Here was a young man in his 20s, married for only three years, with a two-year-old son, and freshly settled in to his recently-inherited estate at Dilston in the Tyne Valley.

Now he was wandering the county, leading a rebellion against King George I, and with everything to lose.

The story of the 3rd Earl of Derwentwater does not end with his execution.

His body was taken by carriage from London to Dilston in Northumberland. As the carriage reached the edge of Durham, onlookers witnessed a remarkable display of the Northern Lights in the sky, which was taken to be an omen.

The home of the Earl's aunt, Lady Mary Radcliffe, is now the County Hotel in Durham and her steward, Francis Dunn, left an account of the lights phenomenon.

The body was taken to Dilston Chapel, minus the heart, which ended up in the keeping of nuns in Paris. In the 19th Century the chapel vault was opened and several of the Earl's teeth were extracted and sold.

The Earl's daughter Anne, born after his execution, married Lord Petre and lived at one of the family homes in Essex, Thorndon Hall.

In 1874, when the Derwentwater estates were sold, the Earl's body was removed from the vault and sent by railway to Thorndon Hall.

Before the body was re-interred, it was examined and the physician noted where the head had been severed from the neck and that teeth were missing.

Five other coffins were taken from the Dilston vault and re-interred at St Mary's RC Church in

Hexham, in whose grounds stands a memorial to the family members.

The clothes which the Earl wore on the scaffold are at the Petre family seat at Ingatestone Hall in Essex. They include his black hat, coat, waistcoat, stockings, a wig of fair hair, part of his shirt with the neck cut away, and the cloth which covered the execution block.

Also at the hall are the prayer book, crucifix, shoes and death mask of the Earl.

Northumberland, featuring 26 locations, to guide the visitor.

Perhaps James Radcliffe realised that his settled life would soon be over and that the trials of the trail were imminent, when in July 1715, the government reinforced a law stating that no Catholic could own a horse worth more than £5. The measure forced James to send his grey stallion to a neighbour for safe-keeping.

When a warrant was issued for his arrest, the Earl went into hiding, and is believed to have stayed at Staward Manor, near Langley, with the Jacobite sympathising Bacon family, and with the Erringtons at Beaufront in the Tyne Valley.

One of the places on the trail is the Derwentwater Cross, erected on the roadside near Langley Castle in the 19th Century as a memorial to James and his brother Charles.

While the Earl lay low, hiding places were used by couriers to leave and collect messages. One such spot on the trail is a row of holly bushes on the Hexham-Slaley road.

The couriers included the two Swinburne sisters from Capheaton Hall and their cousin, Mary Hodgson, whose father Phillip lived at Tone Hall in North Tynedale.

Research for the trail by Frances Dickinson uncovered the extent of Jacobite support in Northumberland.

"Many of the big landowners were supporters of the Stuarts. Northumberland was a very pro-Stuart part of England," she says.

In fact, the 1715 uprising provides one of the theories for the origin of the name Geordies.

The Jacobites expected a surge of support from the workers of Newcastle, but the magistrates barricaded the town gates and declared for King George – hence the inhabitants became known as Geordies.

But it has also been suggested that, because of the level of support the Jacobites were given in the countryside outside Newcastle, the name should have been Jackies and not Geordies.

Other Northumbrian Jacobites included magistrate John Hall, from Otterburn Hall. "Mad Jack Hall", as he was known, joined the rebels on Plainfield Moor and was later executed at Tyburn.

Lord Widdrington, who had family seats at Widdrington Castle on the coast and at Stella Hall near Blaydon, was sentenced to death after the Battle of Preston, but was reprieved on the morning of his execution.

Not so lucky were Northumbrians George Collingwood, of Eslington, who was executed, and Captain John Shafto, of Thockrington, who was shot at Preston.

James and Edward Swinburne, of Capheaton, were taken prisoner at Preston. Edward died in Newgate Prison and James was eventually released. Also freed from Newgate was Thomas Errington, of Beaufront in the Tyne Valley.

Thomas Forster escaped from Newgate with the help of his sister Dorothy.

Charles Radcliffe, brother of the 3rd Earl, was 22 in 1715 and he escaped from Newgate to France. He married the Countess of Newburgh, who was living in Brussels, after impressing her by descending her chimney and appearing in the fireplace to propose.

Charles took part in the 1745 Jacobite rebellion. This time he was not so lucky, and was beheaded on Tower Hill, 30 years after his brother's execution.

It is also believed a standing stone - possibly a Roman altar - in the Warden-Fourstones area was used by couriers while the Earl was hiding at a house in Newbrough, between Hexham and Haydon Bridge.

Finally, the rebels made their move. The Earl and his followers rode to the remote Waterfalls Hill, just off a road which is now the A68 but was at that time the Roman route of Dere Street, to meet up with rebels under Tory MP Thomas Forster, of Adderstone.

On Waterfalls Hill, a Roman milestone near the minor road which leads to Sweethope Loughs, now a popular angling venue, marks where the rebels openly gathered. They rode across Plainfield Moor into Coquetdale, with the Earl spending the night at Rothbury in the Three Half Moons Inn. All that remains of the inn today is its doorway.

Another inn said to have been a regular meeting place for Jacobites was the Red Lion at Stamfordham. Its sole surviving feature, an archway, is also part of the trail.

On October 7, the rebels moved to Warkworth, raising the Stuart flag, where Thomas Forster was appointed to the rank of general.

The legacy of the times can be seen in the form of an inscription across a beam in the Masons Arms in Warkworth, which records that Lord Derwentwater and 40 followers ate at the inn.

From Warkworth, the force moved to Lesbury Common, setting up camp for almost a week overlooking Alnmouth, where the anticipated French landing was to take place. They heard that Lindisfarne Castle had been taken by Tyneside Jacobite sailors, but just as quickly it was recaptured by troops from Berwick.

The rebels decamped to Alnwick, and then Morpeth and Hexham,

Above: Stone archway at
Stamfordham

Left: Three Half Moons Inn at
Rothbury

Derwentwater to George I,
the 26-year-old Earl was
beheaded on Tower Hill in
London in February, 1716.

Frances says: "It is
probably one of the most
dramatic and romantic
episodes in Northumbrian
history.

"The Earl was a young
man, building his massive
mansion at Dilston with
his life stretching ahead of
him, when his close
kinship with Prince James
propelled him into taking
up arms and made him
feel duty-bound to lead the
Northumbrian Jacobites.

"He was drawn into the
event as a victim of
circumstance. He comes
across as a gentle person
who found himself in a
tight corner."

proclaiming King James in
each town. Their next port
of call was Rebel Hill on
Hexhamshire Common,
before they crossed into
Scotland to join the Earl of
Mar's main Jacobite ranks.
The army now numbered
around 2,000. It marched
to Preston, where it was
met by government troops
and defeated.

Revenge was swift. Many of
the ordinary soldiers in the
Jacobite army were hung
or transported. About 200
of their leaders were taken
to London. Despite a
personal plea for mercy
made by Lady

A Northumbrian Jacobite society, The Fifteen, has been set
up. The society aims to promote interest in the Northumbrian
Jacobites, the 1715 rising, and the historic Dilston castle and
chapel site. The society is non-political and non-
denominational, and is entirely an historical and social body
which holds talks, visits, an annual dinner and publishes its
own journal.

Its website is www.northumbrianjacobites.org.uk

Langley Garden Station

On the outskirts of Hexham in Northumberland, what was once a quaint countryside railway station is now a destination for lovers of gardens and art - and tranquillity.

The locomotives, passengers and railway staff are long gone. It is, in fact, more than 50 years since Langley Station closed. But people are steadily returning to enjoy this beauty spot, hidden in woodland with an ambience all of its own.

Langley, on the Hexham-Allendale line, had opened to the sound of band music on March 1, 1869. Now it has a new life under Jane Torday who has nurtured the Garden Station at Langley, which has quietly become established as one of the North-East's most beguiling and off-beat visitor attractions.

Jane took over the wooden station buildings, platform, track bed and two stone bridges. She says: "The original plan was to restore the buildings and have a lovely garden. But then one thing led to another."

There is now an upper garden at platform level. Go down the steps into what Jane calls the sunken garden, developed along the old track bed, which wanders off under the bridges and shades into a

Above: Jane Torday and her foxgloves, and left, taking a break outside the Shed Café

woodland walk. Where once there was only ballast and cinders are now blooms and colour.

"It is a private garden for the pleasure of the public, and it's free," says Jane. "The garden surrounds the enchanting old station. You won't find a garden like it anywhere."

It is a woodland garden with Himalayan poppies,

primulas, hostas and ferns, to reflect Jane's liking of foliage, scented plants like lilies, and what she refers to as a forest of foxgloves. "Because it is sheltered and enriched by years of leaf mould, it is a joy to work in," she says.

The fact that visitors would appreciate a tea or coffee and cake, especially after a woodland walk, led Jane to open the Leaning Shed café. The self-service facility, in a tilting former platelayers' shed, is a contender for the title of the country's tiniest café, thinks Jane.

A 1930s-style railway poster featuring Langley Station by North-East artist Birtley Aris

Left: Inside the Shed Café

She occupies what was the station master's office and two waiting rooms have been combined to provide a base for the courses Jane runs, and a selling space for garden and art items. She says: "My love affair with the station buildings led me to set up gardening courses." They expanded to include craft courses and to cover specialist topics such as singing and cartoon drawing, willow-weaving, gardening for beginners, vegetable growing, garden sculpture, the cottage garden, composting, ferns, designing a Northern garden, Latin plant names, textiles, silk and fibre paper-making, book-binding, origami, hooky and proggy work, watercolour painting and botanical art.

But, of course, people can simply drop in and wander around. Jane says of her visitors: "People come back again and again for a walk, to relax, and perhaps buy plants or pictures.

"The station's strength is that it is idiosyncratic – a secret, hidden, sort of magical small place full of birdsong, and it will never be a big, commercial venture. In a stressful world, people really appreciate all of that."

The garden station has an imposing neighbour in Langley Castle.

When a Scottish army destroyed the hall house at Langley, it did not take owner Sir Thomas Lucy long to wreak revenge.

He was one of the commanders of the English force which shortly afterwards defeated the Scots at the Battle of Neville's Cross, near Durham.

Revenge was one thing. The other was that Sir Thomas needed a new home and this time he built himself a structure which would see off any attackers – Langley Castle.

The 14th Century castle is a landmark on the road from Tynedale to Alston. After a major fire in 1405 it remained empty for centuries until it was restored as a home in the late 19th Century.

The castle became a girls' school, a base for medieval banquets and a private residence.

Then it was spotted in a magazine by Professor of Information Technology, Stuart Madnick, from Boston, US. He bought it and turned it into a hotel. The Grade I listed fortress has four stars, 19 rooms with 7ft-thick walls, and three RAC ribbons for its food.

The Garden Station at Langley is open to visitors from May to November, from 10am-5pm except Mondays, but including Bank Holidays.

Telephone (01434) 684391.

To find the Garden Station, turn off the A69 on to the A686 road to Alston west of Hexham for 2.5 miles and follow the yellow signs after Langley Sawmill.

Langley Castle is off the A686. Telephone (01434) 688888.

Herterton House Gardens

Husband and wife team Frank and Marjorie Lawley have invested the best part of a lifetime in their quest to create the garden of their dreams.

In 1976 they took over a derelict Northumberland farmhouse and an acre of farmyard. To local disbelief, they set about restoring the buildings and working on their vision of a series of gardens surrounding their new home.

The result is one of the most entrancing gardens in the North-East, and it is a true labour of love.

"It has demanded our life, and we have given it. We have no regrets," says Frank.

Visitors to Herterton House and Gardens near Wallington can see around 1,000 varieties of plants – many of them old-fashioned cottage garden specimens.

The couple's passion for plants and enthusiasm for

garden design is underpinned by their artistic backgrounds. Both taught at Newcastle College of Art. Marjorie left teaching in 1970 to concentrate on the gardening, but Frank continued lecturing part time for 36 years in art and garden appreciation.

He says: "The garden is like our art gallery.

The couple combed gardens throughout the North-East and further afield for the old-fashioned herbaceous plants they wanted.

Many had been banished from mansion gardens where vegetables took prominence during the two world wars, or had been discarded as unfashionable.

"Everyone had thrown them away and wanted a dozen modern roses and conifers," says Frank. "We wanted a kind of garden with a wild feel about it."

Today, the visitor passes through a series of gardens, each offering a different experience.

At the front of the house is a formal garden of simple topiary and ferns, planted with native evergreens such as holly, ivy, box and yew.

While the dominant colour is green, there is a succession of bulbs from crocus to crown imperial, madonna lilies and white martagons.

Next is the physic garden, which showcases the importance in the past of economic plants for an isolated farmhouse.

They include medicinal, dye, and poison plants, plus those used in charms and for magical purposes.

The centrepiece is a silver willow-leaved pear tree.

The biggest area is reserved for the flower garden.

The display illustrates the origins of English garden flowers and each bed is themed in separate colours – pink, with companion strips of yellow, cream and white; orange with companions in blue, and the reds, with surrounds of silvery pastel shades.

There are plants such as John-go-to-bed-at-noon, Grim the Collier and Fox and Cubs.

The pink garden features double pink campions, pink chives, and a double daisy from Frank's mother's garden.

At the centre of the orange bed is a lily introduced from Holland 500 years ago and the old brown pansy, Irish Molly.

The newest plot is the fancy garden, which after the flower garden, returns to green and simple geometric patterns.

It is overlooked by a two-storey gazebo with extensive views.

Finally, the visitor enters the nursery area where beds of plants, grown from divisions and cuttings, are for sale.

It is impossible to leave without a living keepsake.

Creating a garden like this is a work of art, a lifetime's work. It is a vision and a sensual experience.

"Our dream was to see if we could make a garden like the wonderful images of beautiful flowers you see in old paintings and tapestries."

The cottage garden style is now a sought-after effect, but shortly after the couple married in 1962, they found themselves with, literally, a cottage garden.

They moved from Newcastle to the cottage between Cambo and Wallington where Marjorie had been born. Her father had been a mason on the Wallington estate.

At Dovecote Cottage, they spent 13 years experimenting with garden design. They immersed themselves in early sources of garden history, including the work of North parson William Lawson and *The Country Housewife's Garden*, published in 1618.

"We started the garden and it was then I knew what I wanted to do," says Marjorie.

Three miles away was their favourite country lane. On that lane was Herterton House, a collection of empty farm buildings. The last farmer had moved out in 1959. Frank and Marjorie decided to move in. At Easter 1976, they began work.

The idea of fashioning a garden at such a neglected site raised many an eyebrow in the local farming community, says Frank.

"It was totally derelict. It was in the days before barn conversions and everyone took a very bleak view of it."

Ten months later they were able to move in. Huge quantities of hardcore and rubble had to be removed from the acre of farmyard.

Frank realised that an 8ft wide, 5ft high bank on the boundary of the site was where soil which had been cleared from the farmyard had been dumped – back it came, by the barrowload.

Another major task was to provide shelter for the gardens, 700ft above sea level. A total of 700 tonnes of local stone was collected by tractor and trailer from within an 11-mile radius of the property and used to build 6ft 6ins high walls.

The first year of the transformation was recorded in the pictures of American Karen Melvin,

who also taught at Newcastle College of Art and specialised in photography.

This left Frank and Marjorie, now in their 60s, with a valuable archive and some of the photographs are on show in the gazebo.

During this time, the couple had to shuttle between Herterton and Dovecote, where they had established a nursery to sell plants.

A crucial factor was a Government job creation scheme which allowed Frank and Marjorie to take on unemployed people for six months or a year over two-and-a-half years.

"It was a tremendous help and we probably couldn't have physically done it without the scheme," says Frank.

Now the garden has

matured, and is still evolving, and 2,000 visitors a year turn up to enjoy it and buy plants from the nursery land.

"If people are inspired by what they see, and gain or discover something from their visit, then that's all right," says Frank.

"The garden is a 12-month a year job, and perhaps a 13-month task as there is always at least a month's work left undone.

"I reckon we work for something like half the minimum wage."

But although the financial returns are hardly substantial, the rewards in other ways are substantial, not least the satisfaction of fashioning a thing of beauty.

"We are totally attached to the garden and life without it is unimaginable," says Frank.

Herterton is signposted off the B6342, which is reached either from Rothbury in the north or from the A696 in the south.

An alternative route is the A1 to Morpeth, then the Scots Gap/Cambo B6343, turning right at the junction with the B6342.

The gardens are open every day from 1.30pm-5.30pm, except Tuesdays and Thursdays.

They are also open by appointment.

Telephone (01670) 774278.

The Prior's Hall at Finchale Abbey

Finchale Priory

In a loop of the River Wear, four miles from Durham City, lies Finchale Priory.

Its story begins with St Godric, who in the early years of the 12th Century set up a hermitage on the riverside near Finchale and later moved to the site of what was to be the priory, building a hut and a chapel.

So remarkable was his life that the account of it must take precedence over that of the priory itself.

He was born around the time of the Norman Conquest in 1066 and became a travelling pedlar, then a merchant with a share in a ship trading with Europe.

By about 1090 he took to the sea and made voyages to Denmark, Flanders and the Mediterranean.

During sailings to Scotland he visited Lindisfarne and the Farne Islands, where he would have learned about St Cuthbert and his life as a hermit.

Some sources say that Godric lived the typical life of a seaman - drinking and fighting - and in one manuscript he was described as a "pirate from the kingdom of England" who is recorded as taking King Baldwin of Jerusalem to Jaffa.

At the age of 20 he had made the first of his pilgrimages to Rome - no mean feat in the 11th Century.

Godric undertook another pilgrimage to the shrine of St James in Compostela in northern Spain, which today is still the destination of many pilgrims.

There followed two more pilgrimages to Rome.

The priory's outlook, facing the River Wear and cliffs topped by woodland, lent itself to an alternative use in the 14th Century – as a holiday home for monks from Durham.

So pretty is the location that in the 13th Century, Prior Hugh of Darlington spent some of his retirement there.

Rules drawn up in 1408 make clear how the holiday retreat operated.

A Prior and four monks living permanently at Finchale were joined every three weeks by another four Durham monks.

On alternate days, two of the holidaying monks had to attend the normal round of services.

The other two, having attended Mass and Vespers, were at liberty to walk "religiously and honestly" in the fields.

Today, visitors can enjoy the same recreation by strolling across the small bridge over the river from the priory to a riverbank walk.

At the age of 40, Godric gave up seafaring and became a hermit.

He lived first near Carlisle in 1104, then joined an older hermit at Wolsingham in Weardale.

Here he had a vision of St Cuthbert, who told him that he would settle at a place called Finchale.

When his older companion died in 1106, Godric made a last pilgrimage to Jerusalem.

He returned to the North-East, where Ranulf Flambard, Bishop of Durham, allowed him to set up home in the Finchale area in 1112.

He was joined by his sister Burcwen, who devoted herself to a life of prayer, and his brother and mother.

The River Wear at Finchale Abbey

They both died and Burcwen was moved to the hospital of St Giles in Durham.

At Finchale, Godric lived a life of self-denial, including wearing a hair shirt under a metal breastplate, using a stone as a pillow, and standing up to his neck in the cold waters of the River Wear to pray.

Said to have a special affinity with wild animals, his reputation as a holy man and visionary spread

and pilgrims began visiting Finchale.

Less welcome visitors were Scots raiders, who gave him a severe beating. He built a church dedicated to St John the Baptist. As he grew older a monk from Durham was sent to live with him.

Godric was 105 when he died on May 21, 1170, and was buried in his Church of St John.

His biographer, Reginald of Durham, was probably

one of two monks who moved to Finchale after Godric's death.

Finchale became a cell of the Cathedral Priory of Durham, and later a priory.

It housed 10 monks, but in 1278 five more arrived to help deal with the pilgrims who were coming to Finchale to see Godric's grave.

More than 200 miracles were claimed at Finchale, and the priory expanded.

A lead ampulla, or small container for holy water often sold to pilgrims at shrines, was found on the site.

By the middle of the 14th Century the Prior's House was renovated, with some of the work apparently being carried out by John Lewyn, the most important provincial architect in medieval England, who also produced Dunstanburgh and Carlisle castles.

After the dissolution of the priory in 1538, it gradually became a picturesque ruin, attracting antiquarian attention in the 19th Century. It is now in the care of English Heritage.

Today, visitors can wander around the priory and trace its history in the substantial remains.

In the Chapter House, where the community would meet every day to discuss priory affairs, there can still be seen stone benches on the side walls and a higher central seat with stone arms for the Prior.

The 15th Century kitchen still has its paved floor, huge fireplace and circular ovens. From the monks' refectory, two sets of stone steps lead down to the undercroft with its impressive stone vaulting.

Even after falling into ruin, Finchale continued to be a place of folklore. The remains of an oriel window in Finchale's Douglas Tower became known as the wishing chair.

The 18th Century antiquary Francis Grose wrote that it "was said to have the virtue of removing sterility and procuring issue for any woman who, having performed certain ceremonies, sat down thereon".

Finchale Priory is north east of Durham, off the A167 Pity Me roundabout. The minor road leading to the priory is opposite Frankland Prison.

The priory is open from April 1-September 30 from 10am-6pm on Saturdays, Sundays and Bank Holidays.

Tel (0191) 386-3828.

Saint Godric's grave was discovered in the 1920s when Sir Charles Peers supervised the clearance of debris from the ruins.

He carried out some excavation work and traced the foundations of Godric's Church of St John. He unearthed a stone coffin where records said Godric's grave lay, against the north wall of the church.

A cross on the ground now marks the spot. The coffin proved to be empty and only a fragment remained of its Frosterley marble lid.

Breamish Valley

It's about an hour's easy drive from the hustle, bustle, noise and urgency of 21st Century life in a packed Tyneside conurbation.

That would take any of the 850,000 people who live in the built up area to the Cheviot Hills and, quite simply, another world.

There, in the Cheviots, are the wild open spaces, the calm and the quiet.

It was the historian G M Trevelyan, whose family seat was at Wallington in Northumberland, who coined the phrase "the land of the far horizons" for this type of expansive and liberating landscape, a phrase which has been perceptively adopted by Northumberland National Park.

In the Cheviots, there is room to wander free from traffic and crowds. The fluting call of the curlew is the only background noise.

But the Cheviots are another world in another

sense, for the valleys and hills contain one of the best-preserved prehistoric landscapes in Europe.

Eleven years of excavations have taken place in the Breamish Valley in the Cheviots, in a joint operation by the National Park, Durham University and the Northumberland Archaeological Group.

The flat grassy stretches alongside the picturesque River Breamish – the haughlands – have, since the Second World War, been a popular picnic spot. But visitors may not have been aware of the weight of history in the hills above.

The valley began to be settled around 4,000 years ago, as evidenced by burial cairns, with farming continuing through the Bronze Age to the creation of a dozen Iron Age hillforts whose defences were built around 2,300 years ago.

There is an astonishing depth of remains in the valley, dating from prehistory through to medieval times. Archaeologist Paul Frodsham says: "The Breamish Valley is, without doubt, one of the most extraordinary archaeological landscapes anywhere in Britain. It has an amazing collection of hillforts, burial cairns, agricultural terraces and Romano-British settlements. You get medieval fields on top of prehistoric fields, Roman period settlements on top of

Visitors to the Breamish Valley can simply enjoy its scenic beauty, riverbanks and wildlife.

But there is also the chance to sample the special experience of walking in a landscape of ancestors.

To stand on the tumbled stone ramparts of Brough Law hillfort, gazing into the jaws of the valley, is to truly tune into the spirit of the place.

The National Park has produced a leaflet guide which enables visitors to take a two-hour walk to Brough Law and the Turf Knowe burial site. A 4.5 mile circular walk takes three to four hours and visits five hillforts.

Setting off from Bulby's Wood car park, the first stop is Brough Law.

Middle Dean's ramparts overlook a dramatic ravine, while Cochrane Pike has views across Coquetdale to Simonside.

Inside Wether Hill there are shallow circular ditches which mark the sites of timber roundhouses.

Ingram Hill is the lowest lying hillfort in the valley and contains the remains of stone buildings which were added long after the hillfort was created.

The trail begs many questions. Were the hillfort defences a reaction to real threats, or were they prestige constructions designed to demonstrate power and status? Why did people choose to live on an exposed hill rather than in the sheltered valley?

Each hillfort seems to sit in its own territory, separated from its neighbour by artificial or natural boundaries. Were these boundaries to stop livestock straying, or were they a territorial response to pressure on land?

Northumberland National Park also offers a leaflet guide to a three-mile route along the bottom of the valley.

The park can be contacted on (01434) 605-555. For the valley's Ingram visitor centre, telephone (01665) 578-248. There are toilets at Bulby's wood car park. The valley is signposted from the A697.

The Breamish Valley Archaeology Project investigated Turf Knowe, a natural ledge and vantage point from which activity up and down the valley could be monitored.

At what became known as Turf Knowe north cairn, archaeologists uncovered a complex burial monument, with the discovery of a food vessel from around 4,000 years ago. A cist, or burial chamber, contained the cremated remains of four to five adults and an iron spearhead, which means the site had been used for at least 2,500 years.

Excavation of the south cairn produced evidence of the use of the ledge as a temporary hunting camp up to 10,000 years ago. Six thousand years later a burial cairn was built with

Iron Age hillforts and Bronze Age settlements. Every time we dig a hole we come across something. It is the time depth and the visual value of the archaeology which makes the Breamish Valley so special.

"There would have been hundreds of people living in the valley around 2,000 years ago. There would have been smoke drifting from roundhouses,

children playing, men hunting, people working in the fields and, no doubt, disagreements between communities. It was a very busy landscape.

"We are providing the archaeological skeleton, but the opportunity is there for people to walk valleys like the Breamish and use their imaginations to envisage what life was like."

Left: Finds from the Breamish excavations

From Wether Hill above the Breamish Valley, there are views to the North Sea, the Cheviot and Simonside Hills.

The hill was chosen for investigation by the Northumberland Archaeological Group.

Between 5,000 and 4,000 years ago, a grave was dug in the hill and two beaker pots were placed alongside the body, with a timber coffin-like box over the pit.

About 2,000 years later, the grave was re-opened for another burial accompanied by three food vessels. It may have been part of a wider cemetery.

There were timber-built roundhouses on the hill summit, then a settlement with timber palisades, and then hillfort defences of ramparts and ditches.

The settlement was abandoned around AD650.

Excavation director Peter Topping says: "By peeling back the layers of evidence from human activity, we now know that people have lived, farmed and been buried on Wether Hill for an almost unbroken record of 8,000 years. This was rarely a silent landscape."

created by clearing the land and building stone walls to increase the depth, thickness and yield of the soil 3,600 years ago. Pollen evidence also indicates that the area was largely cleared of trees 3,500 years ago, probably to provide more land for farming.

A dig at Ingram rectory gardens recovered more than 600 pieces of 12th and 13th Century pottery from what had been cultivated fields, which indicates that people were scattering waste to improve soil fertility.

This was a time of relative peace, but there was no later pottery and from the 14th Century the fields seem to have gone out of use. Scottish raids, a worsening climate and the Black Death seem to have reduced the population and the amount of land under cultivation.

"There have been farmers living and working in the Breamish Valley from around 1500BC to the present day, and all have left evidence of their presence," says Paul.

"Today's farmers are working a landscape inherited from many, many previous generations."

a cremation accompanied by a fine food vessel and jet beads, presumably from a necklace.

A second cist contained incomplete cremations and charcoal from the funeral pyres of three individuals.

Several other cremations were added, including that of a child of about two who, analysis suggested, apparently died after

suffering from meningitis.

At Fawdon Dene, traces of timber roundhouses were revealed, with bones of cattle, pig, horse and dog and evidence of the grinding of grain to make bread and porridge.

A feature of the valley is cultivation terraces dug into the hillsides. Work on terraces on Brough Law showed that they were

Auckland Castle

Auckland Castle in County Durham has long been a centre of prayer as well as power.

The castle is the seat of the Bishops of Durham, and inside, the eyes of the great and good look down from the many portraits of the holders of that grand office from the last 500 years.

The castle in Bishop Auckland stands strategically above the River Wear, which meets the River Gaunless near the castle.

Only the king carried more political weight than the Prince Bishops of Durham. Their power – handy for defending England's northern frontier – included the right to raise an army, pass laws, levy taxes and mint coinage.

Anthony Beck, bishop in 1283, took an active part in Edward I's wars and what is thought to be his

sword is held in the castle.

Many of these activities would have been directed from Auckland Castle, which was the bishops' principal country seat.

William van Mildert, bishop from 1826-36 and the last of the Prince Bishops, founded Durham University in 1832.

He gave what had been the bishop's main residence, Durham Castle, to the new university as its first college. Auckland Castle is now sole residence of the Bishop of Durham and also his office and the diocesean administration centre.

The imposing gatehouse,

A staircase from the castle entrance hall leads to the throne room.

But before that is reached, off an ante-room, is a door to the Victoria Wing, used by Queen Victoria when she travelled north.

She even left a nightdress behind.

There are window views of the Scotland Wing, whose dungeons were used to hold Scottish prisoners in the 15th Century.

Then, through oak double doors, there is the throne room.

The bishop's throne is at the far end of the room, set against an ornate plaster screen. Above is the blue, gold and silver arms of the diocese which includes a crozier and sword, indicating the extra powers given to the Prince Bishops.

They were never needed more than in 1346 when, with the King fighting in France, the Scots invaded and the Prince Bishop raised an army to meet them at the Battle of Neville's Cross, outside Durham.

The 16,000-strong army was amassed in the adjacent Bishop's Park.

The walls of the throne room are covered by the portraits of bishops down the ages.

There are also two carved gilt marble-topped tables which came from the tomb of Thomas a Becket in Canterbury Cathedral.

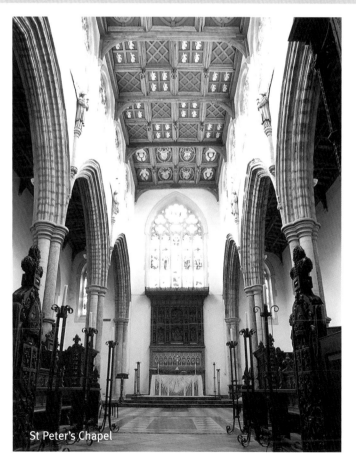

St Peter's Chapel

which fronts Bishop Auckland Market Place, was built in the mid-18th Century and houses a 15th Century clock, while parts of the castle are 800 years old.

Bishop Hugh de le Puiset turned the fortified manor house on the site into a country seat in 1183.

Additions over the centuries have produced an intriguing complex. The castle entrance hall once joined the servants' hall and kitchen with the 12th Century banqueting hall, which had a buttery, wine cellar and minstrels' gallery and was where the bishop dispensed his hospitality.

The original chapel, built by Bishop Beck, was demolished by Parliamentarian and

Off the throne room is the long dining room, whose walls are lined with 13 paintings – each 8ft tall – of Jacob and his 12 sons.

They were painted around 1640 by the Spanish artist Francisco de Zurburan who, under the patronage of King Philip IV, produced works for Spain's American colonies. It is thought the Auckland paintings were destined for the New World.

There are very few Zurburan works in Britain, which makes the presence of Jacob paintings in County Durham extraordinary.

Jacob's sons became the founders of the tribes which formed the people of Israel.

The paintings were thought to have been brought to Britain in 1724 by Sir William Chapman, a director of the South Sea Company, and were bought by Bishop Richard Trevor in 1756 for £124.

The castle's King Charles room was used as a bedroom by Charles I on his journeys to and from Scotland.

His final visit was in 1647 as a prisoner on his way to London.

Puritan Sir Arthur Hazlerigg, who in 1646 bought the castle for just over £6,000.

He used the material to begin building a mansion in the castle grounds. But in the unstable years following the Civil War, fortunes could change quickly and, for Sir Arthur, they did. After the restoration of the monarchy, he found himself in much less agreeable quarters - the Tower of London.

Bishop John Cosin took back the castle in 1660. He demolished Sir Arthur's unfinished mansion and began converting the banqueting hall into the impressive St Peter's Chapel, consecrated in 1665.

Cosin also helped restore churches in the area which had suffered in the Civil War.

In the banqueting hall he raised the roof by 64ft, creating the biggest private chapel in Europe, and decorating the ceiling with richly carved wooden heraldic arms, cherubs and eagles.

Bishop Cosin is buried in the chapel which he did so much to create.

The chapel walls are decorated with the heraldic shields of the many bishops, while the ante-chapel has 49 plaster miniature copies of the sculptures from the frieze of the Parthenon of Athens - the Elgin Marbles - the work of Scottish sculptor John Henning, born in 1771.

The castle hosts weddings, corporate and other events to help pay for the upkeep of the building. Visit it from 2-5pm on Sundays and Mondays, and during August on Wednesdays also. Telephone (01388) 601-627.

Deer Shelter in Bishop's Park

Gateway at Auckland Castle

Next to Auckland Castle is the Bishop's Park – 800 landscaped acres which are open to the public.

Today sheep roam the park, which was enclosed by a wall in the 14th Century. But it was once home to fallow deer and, in the 18th Century, Bishop Trevor built them a stone shelter with battlements, arches and a tower from which picnicking guests could watch the animals.

The park was landscaped by Jeremiah Dixon, who was born in nearby Cockfield. and who was to leave his mark on American history.

Dixon, with Charles Mason, surveyed the boundary between the slavery and non-slavery states which became known as the Mason-Dixon line, giving rise to the term Dixielanders.

Dixon is not the only name associated with Bishop Auckland. Composer Edward Elgar's The Music Makers was first performed in Bishop Auckland. Elgar was a close friend of Nicholas Kilburn, son of a local industrialist.

Comedian and film star Stan Laurel was baptised in St Peter's Church, Bishop Auckland, where his father managed the town's theatre. The family's home in Princes Street and Stan's school still stand.

Also in the town is Latherbrush Bridge, named after a 19th Century beer house where the landlord would shave customers as well as slake their thirsts, and which became known as The Lather Brush.

Bishop Auckland also has a Tenters Street – a reminder of when wet woollen material would be stretched over lines of tenter hooks so it would dry without shrinking – which is where we get the phrase, 'to be on tenter hooks'.

Binchester Roman Fort

An adult and a child stepped into the history books when they walked across the edge of a newly-laid floor at a Roman fort in County Durham while the mortar was still damp.

In a corner of the excavated bath house at Binchester Fort, near Bishop Auckland, their footprints can still be clearly seen after 1,700 years. It is a touching link with a bustling community at a fort which was one of the biggest in northern Britain.

The fort itself covered nine acres and the surrounding civilian settlement – virtually a small town – at least another 30 acres.

Binchester, which has the best preserved example of a military bath house suite in Britain, was big business.

The origins of Binchester, called Vinovia by the Romans, go back to AD79, when it was one of a number of forts on Dere Street. This was the main Roman road from York to Corbridge, in Northumberland, and onward into Scotland, and was built by Julius Agricola, Governor of Britain from AD76-84, as part of the advance into the north.

Left: The Bath House at Binchester Roman Fort

A Roman footprint in the Bath House

Binchester was sited on high ground above a loop in the River Wear, a mile and a half north of Bishop Auckland. It was a good defensive position, and the garrison also guarded the nearby point where Dere Street crossed the Wear.

In fact, Dere Street ran straight through the fort, and an excavated section of it is on display, even down to the stone gutter which ran alongside the route.

The first fort was fashioned from timber and was probably built by the Ninth Legion.

Early in the 2nd Century it was rebuilt in stone by the Sixth Legion. It would have had a stone wall with towers at the corners and four defended gateways,

After the end of Roman rule, the civilian settlement and part of the fort at Binchester continued to be occupied.

Excavations show that sections of the commander's quarters were divided up and used for metalworking and as a slaughter house in the 5th Century.

The bath house also continued in use and there is evidence that the furnaces were heated many times after Roman occupation ended.

But, by the middle of the 6th Century, the fort buildings were quarried for stone and Anglo-Saxon burials were taking place.

At Binchester, a large cemetery has been identified, partly inside the fort, suggesting that it remained an important site as late as the 10th Century.

As Bishop Auckland grew in stature, Binchester became a hamlet around a manor house.

The hamlet homes vanished by the 17th Century and the now-empty Binchester Hall is on the site of the manor house, once owned by the family of the architect Sir Christopher Wren.

But Binchester stayed in the memory for centuries.

In 1552 John Leyland mentions "Romaine Coynes and many other tokens of Antiquite" found in the ploughed fields. In 1586, historian William Camden wrote that Binchester was "well knowne to them that dwell therabout, both in reason of the heapes of rubbish and the reliques of walls yet to be seene and for peeces of Romane coine often digged up which they call Binchester penies."

Excavations took place in the 1970s, but the vast majority of the fort still waits to be uncovered.

Right: The Hypocaust
Far right: a section of Dere
Street at Binchester

with more towers between the corners and the gates.

It was occupied by the Roman army for more than 300 years, and became a supply depot for Hadrian's Wall. The civilian settlement would have catered for the needs of the garrison and the traffic along Dere Street.

From inscriptions found on the site, the identities are known of some of the fort's garrisons. During the 2nd Century it was the base for the Ala Vettonum, a 1,000-strong cavalry unit from central Spain.

"These were unusual in that they had been granted Roman citizenship, because they had obviously distinguished themselves," says David Mason, Durham County archaeologist.

"It was a great honour, and it also meant more pay. So you have this large, well paid garrison. They have to spend their money somewhere – and that is in the civilian settlement."

In Durham City's Fulling Mill Museum of Archaeology, there is a carved stone depicting two figures which was erected by the medical officer attached to the Vettonum cavalry. It is dedicated to the Roman god of health, Aesculapius, and his daughter Salus. It reads: "To Aesculapius and Salus for the welfare of the Cavalry Regiment of vettonians (-)ocomas, doctor, willingly and deservedly fulfilled his vow."

By the early 3rd Century, the garrison had changed to the Cuneus Frisiorum Vinoviensium, which was originally recruited in Holland. This cavalry unit had added Vinovia to its name, almost certainly because of the length of time it was based at the fort.

In the early 19th Century, a farm cart fell into a hole which later turned out to be the hypocaust, or underground heating

system, of the fort's bath house.

In the 1870s, John Proud of Bishop Auckland and the Rev R E Hoopell of Byers Green, near Spennymoor, began excavations of the bath house.

The Binchester bath house, which is protected by a wooden shell, was built around 350 for the exclusive use of the

commanding officer, his family and guests, and was extended towards the end of the 4th Century, by which time it was probably being used by the entire garrison.

The commander's quarters were pretty palatial, with a series of rooms grouped around a central courtyard. The area it occupied was equal to a barrack block which would have housed 80 men. Coins found during excavation showed that the house had been rebuilt around 340.

At Binchester, most bathers would have first used the exercise yard before entering the changing room.

The warm room, which offered a dry heat of about 40C, still has its original concrete floor, and would have been 14ft high with an arched ceiling and painted plaster walls.

The next room, the dry hot room, was next to the bath house furnace, which was fuelled by wood or charcoal, with the heat drawn beneath the floor into the hypocaust space.

The hot air was pulled up through hollow clay tiles behind the walls. Thus heat came through both floor and walls.

After working up a sweat, the next call was to the hot and humid steam room, with its own furnace

heating a water boiler to serve two baths. Water for the baths came through copper and lead taps and pipes connected to the boiler.

The process was completed by a dip into the cold plunge bath in an unheated room.

A total of 88 pillars, which supported the hot room floor, still survive.

Outside the bath house, on one of the foundation stones, is the carving of an animal, thought to be a dog or a bull. This stone would have been out of sight below ground when the bath house was built and is likely to have been a good luck symbol.

The imposing bath house was parallel to Dere Street and must have attracted longing looks from many a sweating squaddie as he trudged along the route.

Binchester is signposted from the A690 Durham-Crook road, from the A688 Spennymoor-Bishop Auckland road and from Bishop Auckland town centre. The fort is open daily from April 15 to September 30 from 11am-5pm and 10am-5pm in July and August. Telephone (01388) 663089.

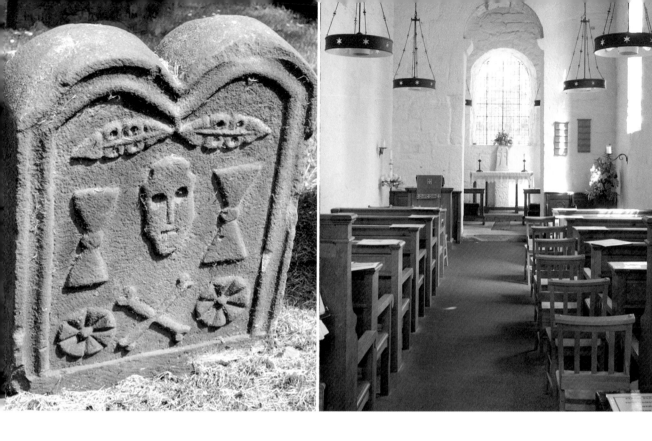

Escomb Church

At the centre of a tiny County Durham village is a late 7th Century church with fascinating tales to tell.

It is claimed that Escomb Church is the oldest complete church in England still in use, and one of the oldest complete Anglo-Saxon churches in the country.

Enter Escomb Church and you stand in a space which has been used for worship for 1,300 years.

It is a building of many messages, from the sun-dial with its apparent pagan overtones to the Roman stones used in the construction of the church, with its Irish Celtic influences.

The roughly circular shape of the churchyard suggests that the church was built on an earlier sacred, or at least important, site near the River Wear.

Stones from the nearby Roman fort of Binchester have been used in the building, including the chancel arch. The arch is believed to have been taken down en bloc from the fort and re-erected in the church.

Other stones show Roman-style diamond-broaching patterns. On the exterior of the North wall is a stone bearing the mark LEG VI – a reference to the Roman 6th Legion and which has been used upside down.

This has given rise to various theories. Were the builders cocking a snook at what had been the splendour of Rome, or did the 6th Legion mean nothing to the builders of

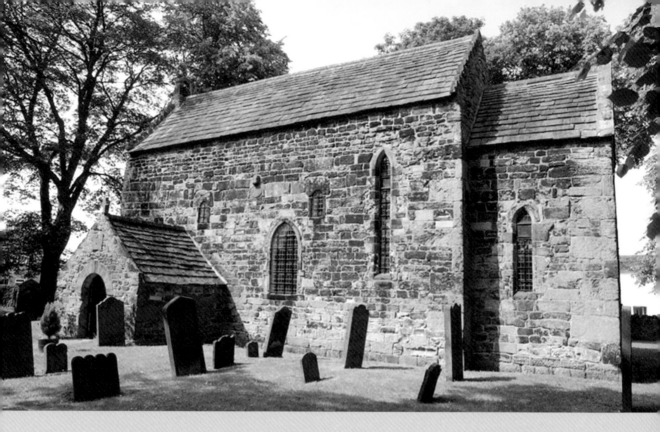

Today, around 3,000 visitors a year seek out Escomb Church and their donations help maintain the ancient building.

Durham University Professor of Archaeology, Rosemary Cramp, says: "Somebody put up something rather special at Escomb at a time when most other churches were made of timber.

"It is a real survivor, and it has a wonderful atmosphere. It is very important nationally because it gives knowledge of what a small church would have been like 1,300 years ago."

Derek Jago, who is a lay reader at the church, says: "There has been worship here for 1,300 years and people often say 'if only the walls could speak'.

"It is a beautiful church with a feeling of stillness and peace."

the late 7th Century?

In 1969, a commendably observant schoolboy noticed an inscription on a Roman stone near a small window. It reads: 'Bono rei publicae nato', which means 'to the man born for the good of the state' and could have come from the base of a statue.

Also used in the building is a rosette stone thought to have been part of a Mithraic altar.

At Escomb, antiquity is everywhere. In the porch are portions of two Saxon crosses.

Behind the altar is a stone cross, thought to date from the 9th Century.

Carved into the walls are consecration crosses from the original dedication of the church.

There are traces of 12th Century fresco work. Much of what was depicted was destroyed during the Victorian period when the church was in decline and parts of the roof were open.

The font is believed to be of 10th-11th Century origin and allowed the total immersion of infants. On its edges are holes for locks from the 13th

A feature of Escomb Church which has sparked most discussion is a sundial high up on the exterior of the south wall.

Dating from the late 7th or 8th Century, it is believed to be the earliest sundial in Britain still to be found in its original setting.

The sundial is surmounted by a beast's head above a serpent.

The need for a sundial indicates the presence of monks who would want to know the correct time of day for prayers. The debate over the sundial centres on what seems to be a mix of Christian and pagan influences.

Prof Rosemary Cramp speculates that it could illustrate evil being contained, with the traditions of a pagan world being given Christian meaning.

Nicholas Beddow, writing from the vicarage at Escomb in the early 1990s, said: "The sundial suggests a faith which was not afraid of pagan symbols."

Century, when it was ordered that fonts should be covered and secured to prevent the taking of holy water for use for superstitious purposes.

Gravestones in the churchyard date from 1628, while a sundial above the porch – one of two on the church – is early 17th Century.

The porch also hosts a display of finds from excavations, including an Anglo-Saxon bead, tweezers and pottery, William III and George III coins and a miner's lodge medal from the local George pit.

It all speaks of long and continuous use, and Escomb Church is certainly a survivor.

It has seen the pledging of the surrounding land in the 10th Century to Danish earls, the upheavals of medieval times, and 19th Century developments such as the pioneering Stockton and Darlington railway with its terminus at nearby Witton Park, and the neighbouring coal mines and iron works. For part of the 19th Century, services were held once a month and Holy Communion every three months, with the clergyman travelling on horseback from Bishop Auckland.

Baptisms were saved up for his attendance and were sometimes held with a funeral.

The closest call for the church came in 1863, when a new parish church was built in the village. The Anglo-Saxon building was reduced in status to a chapel, and fell into a state of neglect.

But in the 1870s two local clergymen, the Rev Hoopell and the Rev Lord, began to raise funds for repairs and in 1880 the church was re-opened by Bishop Lightfoot, who said that "Escomb Church existed when England was not yet England, when Saxons had recently settled on the island, Danes were beginning to harry the coasts and Normans were still undreaded".

A note written after the church's re-opening says: "At the time of the restorations, the skeleton of a very tall man was found in the chancel floor."

How uncertain times had been for the church was revealed when the Bishop told the British Archaeological Association that "the other day I stumbled on a report made by a Rural Dean to my

The timber roof of
Escomb Church

parson. Happily things are now changed, high and low, rich and poor, love their old church.

"They talk and think about these ancient Saxon stones which have such a wondrous attraction, and such mighty stories to tell.

"The restoration has caused the thoughtless to think and driven idle loungers, who were wont to make its God's acre a playground, elsewhere."

In 1970 the building once again became a parish church, while a year later the Victorian church was demolished.

Escomb is three miles west of Bishop Auckland in County Durham.

Guides are on duty at weekends and most afternoons during the summer.

At other times, a notice at the church entrance gives the address of a nearby house from which the church key can be collected.

For details call (01388) 458358.

predecessor in which he states that it (the Saxon Church) is in a sad state of decay, and would be better removed."

But the church remained and the tide turned. An 1881 guide said: "A rough population dwelt hereabouts, who respected neither Church nor

Rothley Castle and Winter's Gibbet

As a legacy of its centuries as a frontier zone, the North-East has an array of fortifications, from defended farmhouses to towers and castles.

By the middle of the 18th Century there was hardly a need for any more.

But Sir Walter Blackett of Wallington in Northumberland couldn't resist adding to the line up.

He built a mock castle, and later a fort, on crags on his estate, and today they still stand as picturesque curiosities.

Sir Walter inherited his uncle's estate at Wallington in 1728. It was mostly moorland and fell, with few trees and crossed by cart tracks.

His thoughts turned to drawing up a plan for major improvements and in under 30 years he had accomplished his great task.

He built bridges, roads which could take stagecoaches, created fields and farmsteads, and planted woodlands.

He also turned to the leading architect Daniel Garrett, who began the remodelling of Wallington house in 1738.

Sir Walter was not afraid to dip deep into his pocket for his grand scheme. After

all, his expenses in his election campaign as an MP in 1741 totalled a staggering £6,319.

After shaping the landscape around his home, he switched his attentions to Rothley Crags, to the north of his estate, around which he began to fashion an enclosed deer park.

The park was bounded by two new roads – the Hexham-Alnmouth and the Morpeth-Elsdon turnpikes, which met at Rothley Crossroads.

Rothley Park would

Raw Bastle

provide a link between the tamed landscape of the Wansbeck Valley and the wilder moorland. Sir Walter also created Rothley Lakes by damming a stream, and surrounded the feature with extensive woodland planting.

One of his pleasures after dinner was to drive to the lakes, which are now bisected by the B6342 Wallington-Rothbury road.

The western part of the lakes is run as a nature reserve by the National Trust.

The walls of the deer park, which survive although reduced in height, would have been a big job in themselves. But by 1774 they must have been complete, as there is a record of Squire Widdrington of Longhorsley providing 30 deer to help stock the park.

Another survivor is a drinking trough for the deer, which was cut into the rock, being filled with rainwater channelled from a natural outcrop.

Such a prominent feature as Rothley Crags were a natural choice for a defended settlement and there are the remains of a prehistoric hilltop enclosure. Sir Walter thought along the same lines and in the 1740s Garrett produced a design for the mock Rothley Castle.

It would have been both an eye-catcher for estate visitors and travellers, and a venue for excursions for Sir Walter's guests.

The castle, which still sits today on top of the crags, includes a central stone tower, with walls running to the north and south to join flanking towers.

Originally, there were battlements, while some of the cruciform slits can still be seen.

Stone figures, brought to Wallington from the demolition of Bishopgate and Aldersgate in London – including the griffins' heads now in front of the house – were used to embellish the castle, along with a whale's jawbone which was fixed to the walls.

Not far from Rothley crossroads is Gallows Hill.

It is a taste of what awaits further along the road from the junction towards Elsdon.

At Steng Cross, which marks the highest point of the road overlooking Harwood Forest, is Winter's Gibbet.

The stone base of the ancient cross on what is an old drove road stands next to the gibbet, which today is a replica of the original.

Suspended from the scaffold is a block, which represents the head of William Winter.

The gallows were also erected to face the general direction of the scene of the crime for which Winter was executed.

Taking the B6341 road from Elsdon to Rothbury leads to the murder site. On the hillside, up a minor road from the tiny Billsmoor pull-in, is The Raw bastle, at the farm of the same name.

The bastle, or fortified farmhouse, is one of three in the immediate vicinity.

The view to the south is over the rugged high ground of Darden Pike, Darden Lough and Rumbling Cleugh, an area which still retains an air of wildness.

It was the outlook which widow Margaret Crozier, who lived at The Raw bastle, would have seen daily. But in 1791 she was murdered in her bastle.

On the basis of observations by a shepherd boy who had met Winter and his companions Jane and Eleanor Clark the day before, the three were arrested for the crime.

They were hanged in Newcastle. The bodies of the women were sent to the Surgeon's Hall for medical dissection.

Winter's body was gibbeted in chains at Steng Cross.

Both the practice and the background illustrate the harshness of the times.

The executioner, William Gardner, had himself been sentenced to death for stealing sheep. After he carried out the hangings his own sentence was reduced to seven years transportation.

In 1791 Winter had been released after serving a seven-year imprisonment, during which both his father and brother had been executed for the offence of breaking and entering.

The father of Jane and Eleanor Clark had also been hanged on a charge of burglary.

The shepherd boy, too, did not live long. He moved out of the area for fear of gypsy reprisals, but died aged 20 or 22 after returning home.

A stone staircase in the castle tower led to a platform to allow visitors to enjoy the views.

The crags had previously been used for more serious purposes. The inner part of the prehistoric enclosure had been pressed into service as a defendable area to protect livestock from raiding Reivers.

Rothley Crags were also part of a chain of beacons to give warning of impending attack from the north.

There is the possibility that

Codger Fort

Tower at Rothley Castle

the castle may not have simply been a folly and conversation piece. In 1745 the Jacobites had invaded, and Rothley could have served a defensive role if necessary.

Whatever, Sir Walter was not finished and in 1769 the astronomer Thomas Wright of Durham delivered a design for Codger Fort, a mile north of Rothley, on a craggy outcrop overlooking Rothley Lakes. The stone, triangular bastion looks down on the road to

Rothbury. Apparently, six cannon were obtained from Chatham Dockyard and installed at the fort.

In 1879, the land was sold and remained in private hands until the National Trust was able to buy the Grade Two-star listed castle and 242 acres, backed by a generous bequest from supporter Ann Dawson, who had stipulated that the money had to be used to buy land or property in Northumberland. The acquisition included half of the original deer park.

The formal woodland plantations are of exactly the same form as is shown on a map of 1777.

Harry Beamish, National Trust regional archaeologist, says: "Rothley Castle was about 18th Century fun and games, and it would also have given views to the

coast and of the estate which Sir Walter was improving.

"It was a huge undertaking, but it was seen as a duty to take unproductive land and improve it. As well as the economic side of the development, having a deer park would have been seen as a mark of status.

"There was a mania for landscaping and if you had the resources it would have been quite fun.

"Taking a romantic setting and building the castle in it was improving on nature. The castle was intended to be seen from afar and for people to stop and comment on it."

More than 250 years later, they still do.

Water wheel

Brewery shaft

Waterfall at Nenthead

Nenthead Mines

High, and to all intents hidden, in the hills of the North Pennines is Nenthead.

At 1,500ft it is said to be the highest village in England and its geographical peculiarities do not end there.

Although just inside Cumbria, Nenthead is at the crossroads where the county meets both Northumberland and County Durham.

The North Pennines has long been a stronghold of Methodism, and Nenthead's Primitive Methodist chapel, now a house, is the highest building in England to have been used for worship.

St John's Church in the village, built in 1845, is of course the highest church in use in the country. Today, surrounded by open moorland, it is a quiet and remote village. But in the 19th Century things were very different. The place bustled with activity.

Anywhere between 1,000 and 2,000 people worked in the mines in the hills. The workings in the valley of the River Nent, a tributary of the South Tyne, became one of the largest and the most productive lead mining sites in Britain. It is estimated that there are almost 100 miles of tunnels and workings linked to the Nenthead lead mines. They extend over the moorland, with tunnels connected to mines in neighbouring valleys.

Rising up the valley from the village is the Nenthead Mines Heritage Centre, which covers 200 acres of lead and zinc mining and processing remains.

Once this was regarded as a bleak and derelict area. But perceptions change. It is now viewed as an

A shaft on the Nenthead site is a link to one of the strangest and least known man-made features in the North-East.

The 382ft deep Brewery Shaft is connected to the Nent Force Level, a tunnel which was excavated at the bottom of the Nent Valley and which runs for four and a half miles underground to the town of Alston.

Begun in 1776, it took 63 years to complete and cost £81,000.

The Brewery Shaft is the last of nine shafts down to the Nent Force Level.

It is enclosed by a building and surrounded by a viewing platform.

A press of a button and the room is plunged into darkness. Another button and a string of lamps lining the shaft are switched on to give a breathtaking view into the depths.

The Nent Force Level was driven to find new mineral veins and also to drain the mines in the area. Only one money-making vein was found.

By the early years of the 19th Century the flooded tunnel had become something of a visitor attraction. Mine agent Thomas Sopwith, who lived and worked in nearby Alston from 1824, wrote of the Nent Force Level:

"It is navigated in boats 30ft in length which are propelled by means of sticks projecting from the sides of the level and thus may be enjoyed the singular novelty of sailing a few miles underground and beholding in perfect safety the various rocks and the numerous veins which it intersects.

"As a number of candles are usually taken up, a variety of beautiful effects may be produced by leaving short pieces of them burning at intervals.

"The reflection of them in the water presents a fine spectacle and some idea is afforded of the vast extent of the level by the receding vista of lights."

Mackenzie's History of Northumberland of 1825 states: "The level of Nent Force is a stupendous work. Strangers may be accommodated with boats and guides by application at the Lowbyer Inn near Alston.

"Those who have the curiosity of taking a subterranean sail must be highly satisfied with the singularity of the scene. When accompanied by a band of music, the effect is beyond description."

In 1881, a book called North Country Sketches by Newcastle's John William Allan was published.

Allan toured the northern counties, writing as he went, and persuaded two brave souls from Alston to take him into the Nent Force Level in a boat with candles stuck to the sides and accompanied by a howling bulldog. Allan wrote: "We seemed to be so far away from things of the earth and were ploughing through its very bowels.

"There must have been enormous quantities of carbonic acid gas gathered and this, with the absence of oxygen, caused a feeling of great drowsiness."

important industrial heritage site and one with great educational and tourism potential.

Most of the 200 acres are designated as a Scheduled Ancient Monument and there are two sites of special scientific interest.

The site is run by the North Pennines Heritage Trust, which has carried out archaeological surveys, restored mining buildings and is dedicated to telling the story of what happened in the valley.

The site's former engineering workshops now house the Nenthead Story Exhibition, and what were the joinery workshops and timber yard are now the Trust's offices.

What drove the whole show was the water running down from the hills.

The North Pennines landscape is laced with hushes. These channels were created by damming burns and then releasing a torrent to strip off vegetation and rock to expose veins of lead ore.

Restoration work has been carried out on miles of

leats - stone-lined channels in the ground to funnel the water - and launders, which are wooden versions above ground.

The site's biggest exhibit, the Power of Water, is designed to show visitors just that. People can pull levers to release water which powers water wheels, with each working in a different way.

The Alston Moor deposits at Nenthead were worked in the 17th and 18th centuries by small companies and individuals before being acquired by Greenwich Hospital in London.

The wealth won from the lead mines helped pay for the grandeur of Greenwich.

Many of the smaller leases were sold to the Quaker-run Ryton Company on Tyneside which in 1704 merged with a southern counterpart to form the London Lead Company.

The company began operations in Nenthead in 1745 and continued until 1882.

Miners formed partnerships, often six to eight men, and usually from friends and family.

They struck deals with mining agents to work certain sections and, with the men having to pay for their own tools, candles, gunpowder, haulage and processing of the ore for smelting, it was a gamble on whether their chosen site would be profitable.

On the washing floors, the ore was broken into small pieces and water was used to separate the lead ore from the rock. The work was mostly carried out by boys over 12.

With its Quaker background, the company did attempt to ease the hardships faced by its workers.

Many miners had smallholdings where vegetables could be grown and some livestock kept. The company also bought land to let as allotments.

It bought goods in bulk and transported them to its warehouse so as to keep the costs of purchase low for the workers.

But in five famine years from 1815 the company had to dole out corn at cost. One mine agent's journal of 1817 reads: "March 17: A supply of oatmeal delivered to the workmen. They are many of them in a state of starvation."
In 1817 the company set up a subscription welfare fund for sickness, accident and death benefits, appointed a doctor and in 1819 built a school.

In 1825 it went one better when it built a model village of cottages, gardens, market hall, clock tower and shop.

A reading room followed in 1833, with one of the first free libraries in England. Today it is the village over-60s meeting room.

After the London Lead Company ceased operations, the Belgian Vielle Montagne Zinc Company moved in from 1896 to 1949, bringing Belgian, German and Italian workers.

Minerals like fluorspar had been thrown away by the lead miners. But by the middle of the last century it had become a usable commodity and soil heaps were worked for the material until 1965, when Nenthead finally became as quiet as the encircling moors and hills.

To reach the Nenthead Mines Heritage Centre, turn off the A69 on to the A686 to Alston and then take the A689 Alston-Stanhope road.

Alternative routes are the minor road off the A686 after Whitfield to Ninebanks and Carr Shield and then Nenthead. This is an attractive moorland drive. Another route is the B6303 via Allendale, Allenheads and Cowshill to join the A689.

The centre is open from Easter to the end of October daily from 10.30am-5pm. There is a shop and café. The site is open at all times to groups by prior appointment. Tel: (01434) 382037.

Wheels operated wooden machinery which crushed ore, and provided the counterweight to lift buckets full of stone.

The biggest water wheel at Nenthead was 50ft in diameter and the deep cleft which accommodated it can still be seen at the back of what was the site's smelt mill.

It was built in 1847, at a cost of £7,000, to drive the pumps for a condenser.

It was known that during smelting, lead particles were being lost up chimneys and along the flues which served them. The condenser drew the gases through a series of water chambers which caused the lead to drop to the bottom for collection. Flues and chimneys were also scraped and the deposits were re-smelted to recover still more lead.

The smelt mill was in production for 160 years and grew to have six ore hearths, a slag hearth, four furnaces and a de-silvering house.

A system for separating silver from lead ore was devised by local man, Hugh Lee Pattinson, in 1833. Ten tons of silver was recovered at Nenthead, which also processed 190,000 tons of zinc and 300,000 tons of lead ore.

By today's standards, the smelt mill was a health and safety nightmare. Heat from the furnaces, which were kept going day and night, was immense and there were hazards like molten lead, dust and toxic fumes from the lead.

The ore also contained arsenic and mercury. The miners working in damp, close conditions underground, did not often live past 50 or work beyond 45. Many suffered from "black spit" - a condition caused by inhaling dust. The life expectancy of a smelter was even less.

Buildings which have been restored include the barrack house, which housed itinerant miners. They left carvings on the barrack door and flagstones which front the building.

The Carr's Level mine has been re-opened to the public. Visitors can tour the workings, dating from the mid-18th Century, with a guide and see how the miners followed the veins.

At the end of the tour they emerge at a small waterfall. As if they need reminding, it is a case of water, water everywhere...

The Engine House at Shildon

Blanchland

For the streams of visitors drawn to the picturesque village of Blanchland, there are few clues that it was once the centre of a major industry.

But production of lead ore in the Derwent mines around the village totalled about 40,000 tonnes between 1845 and 1883.

There were mines at the hamlet of Shildon, near Blanchland, in 1475 when they were granted by Edward IV to his brother the Duke of Gloucester.

A walk or short drive from Blanchland to Shildon reveals the dramatic ruin of Shildon Engine House on the edge of woodlands in the valley of the Shildon Burn.

Once known locally as Shildon Castle, the imposing structure is sited alongside a shaft which explored the Old Shildon ore vein to a depth of 600ft.

The pumping engine for the building was ordered from Birmingham and was laboriously transported by canal, sea, river boat and teams of horses.

Blanchland Village Square

Over Heatheryburn Moor and Nookton Fell from Blanchland is Allenheads.

The village was also a centre of lead mining, and Thomas Sopwith was mine agent.

Sopwith kept a diary which amounted to 168 volumes, and organised a display of a case of 2,000 mineral specimens from the area at the Great Exhibition in the Crystal Palace in London in 1851.

The collapse of the mining industry saw the population of the Allen Valley fall from 6,000 in the mid-19th Century to just above 2,000 in 1900.

In 1987, the Allenheads Trust was set up to revive the village, which is now a pretty cluster around the 18th Century Allenheads Inn, heritage centre and the Hemmel cafe.

In the churchyard of St Cuthbert in Allendale is a monument to Isaac Holden. Its inscription speaks of the "esteem and respect" in which he was held, with 600 people subscribing to the memorial.

Isaac Holden was born in 1805 in the West Allen Valley, the son of a lead miner. As a boy of eight he started work on the mine, washing floors, and later became a miner himself. But he lost his job when the Kiersleywell mine closed and he became a travelling tea seller in the North Pennines.

In the course of his rounds, Isaac, a Methodist, devoted himself to doing good works and raising funds for that purpose. He paid off the debts of chapels, helped set up a savings bank and clothing fund for poor women and children, provided a fresh water supply and gathered money for a hearse for the West Allen.

The mine in which Isaac worked runs under the Ninebanks youth hostel, itself a former miners' lodging shop.

Roger Morris, secretary of the Friends of Ninebanks Youth Hostel, was behind the creation of the circular 36-mile walk called Isaac's Tea Trail.

Beginning and ending at the hostel, its aim is to showcase the North Pennines.

Roger says: "Isaac's life was turned upside down when he lost his job at the mine and he began selling tea door-to-door.

"He became a one-man fundraiser and community worker. He was quite a remarkable character."

Roger believes the trail introduces people to what makes the North Pennines so special.

"It is different to anywhere else. There is such a variety of history, combined with wildlife and geology.

"You never get to the bottom of it all. I just love it."

There were no sightseers in the lead mining days. The historian William Hutchinson wrote of Blanchland in 1776: "This place looks truly like the realm of mortification ... the buildings which are standing are now inhabited by the poor people who are perhaps employed in the lead mines.

"The distress and rugged appearance of the village being most deplorable."

John Wesley, blazing the trail of Methodism, preached in Blanchland churchyard in 1747 and described the village as "little more than a heap of ruins".

Yet today, visitors arrive at a village which the writer of a 1951 history of Blanchland described as "almost Mediterranean in appearance".

He mused that while many villages are strung out along roads or circle a green, most of the buildings in Blanchland are grouped around an L-shaped piazza, with an impressive 15th Century gateway into which is set the village post office with its white Victorian post box.

The setting of the village is enhanced by the fells which rise steeply on all sides and the River Derwent that separates Blanchland in Northumberland from County Durham across the 18th Century bridge.

The village owes its change in fortunes to Lord Crewe, Bishop of Durham, who bought the lands in the early 18th Century.

When he died in 1721 the estate was run by the Lord Crewe Trustees, who in the mid-18th Century set about creating a model village out of the ruins of Blanchland Abbey.

On his visit Wesley observed: "There seems to have been a large cathedral church by vast walls which still remain."

A number of buildings follow the outlines of the

The Lord Crewe Arms, Blanchland

abbey complex. And indeed, if the word Mediterranean has been used in conjunction with Blanchland in the past, then it could be argued that the village in fact had its origins in Germany.

It was there early in the 12th Century that a canon called Norbert had a profound religious experience which inspired him to build an abbey and found the Premonstratensian Order.

In 1165 they established Blanchland Abbey in what was then a very remote corner of the North-East and which is still out-of-the-way.

The order's monks wore white cassocks, cloaks and caps. Their holdings became known as the White Land, or Blanchland.

The abbey knew hard times, and suffered in the Scottish wars. In the 14th Century the abbey petitioned Edward III for relief, having lost 140 acres of crops and 500 sheep.

Today, the Lord Crewe Arms occupies the land of the abbey cloister and its tower is probably what was the abbot's lodging.

A row of cottages is on what was the abbey refectory, or dining room.

The Church of St Mary the Virgin, next door to the Lord Crewe Arms, was built by the trustees in 1753 around the original monastic church.

It includes a circular pillar thought to have been part of the 1165 church, and the sculpted heads of Edward III, who stayed at Blanchland in 1327, and Philippa, his queen.

The church served a village whose population in 1861 was 265, covering 45 trades.

One of the few signs of a lead mining past are the decorative L-shaped stones around the village, which supported the winding engine at the nearby Ramshaw mine.

View of Mitford Church from the castle

Mitford Castle

Mitford today is a peaceful, pretty and highly agreeable place to live.

But about 700 years ago the neighbours from hell made sure the Northumberland village, near Morpeth, was a place to avoid.

Mitford Castle is now a picturesque ruin atop its sandstone knoll overlooking the River Wansbeck.

But in 1315, following the defeat of Edward II at Bannockburn, the castle was the base of the infamous Mitford Gang, headed by Sir Gilbert de Middleton of Cramlington and Hartley, and his sidekick Walter Selby.

Selby, whose property included Biddlestone in Coquetdale and a fortified tower in Seghill, was described as "both a robber and a warrier".

As if Northumberland did not have enough to contend with in terms of Scottish wars and raids, the Mitford Gang inflicted still more mayhem on the county.

They pillaged farms and took captives for ransom, holding them at Mitford Castle.

But in 1317 it was a case of a set of prisoners too far, when the gang laid in wait at Rushyford in County Durham and ambushed

When the Mitford family returned to their namesake location, they opted not to live in the castle, but to build a manor house opposite.

Today, the only inhabited part of the house is the former kitchen wing, which was converted into a home in the 1960s.

The tower, once the entrance to the manor house, survives as the ultimate garden feature. It bears the arms of the Mitford family – who still own it – and the date 1637.

Of the manor house's main block, one wall with its fireplaces is exposed.

Another manor house relic gives a whole new meaning to the saying 'why keep a dog and bark yourself'. The house had a treadmill operated by a dog in the manner of a hamster wheel.

The treadmill turned a spit on which meat was roasted in front of the fire.

The wheel is now on show in the Chantry building in Morpeth.

Bishop of Durham-elect Lewis de Beaumont.

He and his brother had been on their way to Durham Cathedral for his consecration. Instead, they, too, ended up captive in Mitford Castle.

An account reads that Sir Gilbert "kept many of his neighbours in the castle of Mitford at a heavy ransom". But in December 1317, the castle was taken, and Gilbert was carted off to the Tower of London.

He was hung, drawn and quartered and the four sections of his body sent to Newcastle, York, Bristol and Dover.

Monastic records say: "So ended a year that was barren of every crop but misery when Northumberland, wasted by the Scots, and reduced to poverty by its own outlaws, lay between the hammer and the anvil."

Walter Selby escaped to Scotland and when the Scots captured Mitford Castle in 1318, King Robert Bruce placed him in charge of the fortress.

Selby sat it out for three years before surrendering himself and the castle to the Sheriff of Northumberland.

He also ended up in the Tower, but was freed and fought in the Scottish Wars on the English side.

Alas, his luck ran out, for he was taken prisoner by Bruce, then executed.

His tower at Seghill went to the Delavals who, in 1441, completed the circle when they sold it to the Mitford family, who in turn kept it for another 300 years.

The Mitford family owned land west of Morpeth

Mitford Castle

One of the seasonal sights in Northumberland is the carpet of snowdrops around Mitford Church.

The Church of St Mary Magdalene has, like the castle opposite, a long history. It has been damaged – especially by a fire in 1705 – and rebuilt several times.

By the middle of the 12th Century, it was already a notable church.

The Rev Isaac Nelson, believed to be a relative of Horatio, became vicar in 1759 and rebuilt the vicarage.

But as he was returning home in March, 1772, he was drowned after falling off the river stepping stones at Mitford.

The church was restored in the 1870s by the squire of Mitford, Colonel John Philip Osbaldeston Mitford, at a cost of at least £10,000.

The church grounds are the last resting place of several of the Mitford family. One of the memorials is to the Rev George Mitford, eldest son of Capt C J Mitford, who died at sea in 1866, aged 49, while on passage from Bombay to Suez. It also commemorates his wife, Sarah, who died at sea the following year.

According to the Mitford Historical Society, William Mitford wrote a five-volume History of Greece, published in 1808.

John Mitford died in the London workhouse in 1831, having served in the Royal Navy under Nelson. He wrote a song called The King is a True British Sailor.

Mary Mitford, who died in 1855, wrote Our Village and Recollections of a Literary Life.

But Edward Ledwich Mitford, who was squire until his death in 1912, aged 101, is of Boys' Own stature.

He worked in Ceylon – now Sri Lanka – in the civil service and, astonishingly, travelled there by horse and foot, writing about his adventures in An Overland March to Ceylon.

The best known Mitfords were the Mitford girls – the daughters of the Second Lord Redesdale. Nancy, born in 1904, wrote Love in a Cold Climate and The Pursuit of Love.

Diana was married to a Guinness heir but became the mistress and then wife of Oswald Mosley, founder of the British Union of Fascists in the 1930s.

Unity Valkyrie Mitford was a personal friend of Adolf Hitler. When the Second World War broke out, she shot herself in the head, but survived and had her hospital bills paid for by Hitler.

Jessica declared herself a Communist and ran off to support the cause in the Spanish Civil War. She emigrated to the US, joined the US Communist Party and wrote The American Way of Death.

Deborah became Duchess of Devonshire.

A photographic record of life in and around Mitford was built up from 1898 to 1934 by the vicar, Canon Roderick McLeod. His extensive collection of glass slides is held by the Northumberland Records Office.

Second World War pill box at Mitford Castle

before the Norman Conquest. A daughter married Robert Bertram, whose son William was established in his timber castle at Mitford by 1115 and later founded Brinkburn Priory, near Rothbury.

Roger Bertram had completed the stone castle on the site by 1215. It was used as a base by King John during his vengeance operation against the Northern noblemen who had sided with the Scottish King Alexander, who had besieged Mitford.

In the 13th Century, a five-sided keep - the only one in the country - was

added to the castle.

The castle passed to the Earl of Pembroke, who was killed during a tournament organised to celebrate his wedding.

By 1327, Mitford was described as "the site of a castle wholly burned".

Given its turbulent history and later treatment as a source of building stone, it is surprising how much has survived.

Survival was not an option for one of the castle prisoners. He carved the words "Captivus Morior" meaning "I die a prisoner" on the stone steps of the vaults used as a jail.

Once a defended site, always a defended site, and today a listed Second World War pill box stands next to the castle.

The Mitford family acquired the castle in the 17th Century and were represented in the village until the early 1990s, when the castle and 3,000 acres were bought by Shepherd Offshore, which appointed Newcastle architect Cyril Winskell to address the historical aspects of the land.

English Heritage has given grant aid to help consolidate the ruin and Cyril says: "The castle is a national treasure. It is enormously important historically and architecturally."

Aydon Castle

Aydon and Prudhoe castles

Buying a property has always had its risks - will you settle, are the neighbours friendly, and will home improvements prove a good investment?

It's a fair bet similar questions were going through the mind of Robert de Reymes at the end of the 13th Century.

He was from a family of Ipswich merchants who were looking to go up in the world. They were friendly with the de Gosbeck family, who through marriage had acquired land in Northumberland - including Aydon Castle, near Corbridge in the Tyne Valley.

Aydon, now in the care of English Heritage, is tucked away a mile and a half from Corbridge, overlooking the picturesque and steep valley of the Cor Burn.

The seclusion makes it a delightful spot. But it was not always so peaceful.

Back to the de Reymes. They saw the opportunity to become Northern barons by purchasing the neglected de Gosbeck estates in Northumberland. Aydon was apparently not in the best of shape and Robert de Reymes set about sinking his Suffolk money into the building.

Left: The Granaries at Corbridge
Right: Remains of Fountain House

The inhabitants of castles like Aydon and Prudhoe were by no means the first to have to deal with the dangers of life on the frontier.

A short distance from Aydon is Corbridge Roman site, which began life as a fort on the northernmost edge of the empire and ended up as a garrison town just behind the front line.

It is a strangely evocative place. Many thousands have walked and ridden along the Stanegate – the main road through the site.

At its highest point the road surface dates from the 4th Century. Beneath are layer after layer of surfaces which continue for several metres to the first route in AD90.

The first fort was part of a frontier patrol road. After the building of Hadrian's Wall the fort, two-and-a-half miles behind the new barrier, was rebuilt.

By the 3rd Century Corbridge had become more like a town. Evidence suggests life there had its scares.

By the roadside are the remains of granaries on which, it seems, work was interrupted – probably by an invasion of hostile tribes from the North known to have taken place in AD180.

Today, the bases of porticoes which once sheltered the loading bays of the granaries are still in place.

Next door is the fountain house. A closed aqueduct brought water to an aeration tank where contact with the air revived its freshness. On either side were statues and in front was a stone trough from which water was drawn for public use.

The town was much more extensive than today's visible remains suggest and extends to 27 acres under surrounding fields.

With its shops, temples and other attractions, it would have been an attractive leave centre for the troops on Hadrian's Wall.

After the Roman occupation it became a quarry for stone for Hexham Priory, Corbridge parish church and many other buildings.

But excavations have produced a wealth of finds to piece together life during the town's heyday, which are on display in the site museum.

In 1964 the remains of a wooden chest were unearthed, containing pieces of body armour, spear heads, catapult bolts, tools, scabbards, horse harness and many other objects.

Newcastle University's Lindsay Allason-Jones, who had written a book called Roman Woman, says: "There would have been merchants, traders, soldiers, farmers and veterans at Corbridge.

"The fields are full of streets laid out in a grid pattern with lots of shops, with people making and selling things.

"It would have been very cosmopolitan, with people from all over the Roman world, with every colour of skin and language.

"There was even a Greek priestess at Corbridge dedicating altars."

The Gateway at Prudhoe Castle

Kitchen at Aydon Castle

But his timing could not have been worse. His arrival coincided with renewed fighting in Northumberland with the neighbours - the Scots.

Corbridge suffered badly and was attacked in 1296 and again the next year - when de Reymes began his work at Aydon - then on another four occasions up to 1322.

In 1305, de Reymes had been granted a licence to fortify Aydon. But in 1315 it surrendered to a Scots army which did not treat it kindly and engaged in traditional pillaging and burning.

To make matters worse, de Reymes had been captured, probably at the Battle of Bannockburn, and was eventually ransomed.

He returned to find order had collapsed in the wake of the Bannockburn defeat and English rebels had seized Aydon.

Robert died in 1323 and an effigy in Bolam church in Northumberland is almost certainly him.

The constant conflict meant that at his death, his manor house at Bolam had been burned by the Scots, 100 acres of arable land was untilled, 12 acres of meadow and six acres of pasture had no animals on them and 10 farmhouses and cottages had no tenants.

Another of Robert's manors at Shortflatt had been burned and 200 acres were waste.

Prudhoe Castle

If Aydon just about qualifies as a castle, then nearby Prudhoe is very much the genuine article.

Prudhoe fits the traditional, towering castle image and with just cause, as it commands a strategic crossing of the River Tyne and the east-west route from Carlisle to Newcastle.

It is the third major castle along the Tyne after Tynemouth and Newcastle.

Unlike Aydon Castle, which has retained its sense of rural retreat, Prudhoe has become increasingly surrounded by modern urban development. But that is not to detract from its dramatic position, on a steep-sided spur 150ft above the river.

This was a natural defensive site, with streams having cut deep denes on either side of the spur.

Archaeological excavations suggest the site was occupied in the mid-11th Century with timber buildings protected by a palisade.

There had been several attempts by Scottish kings to take over Northumberland, but the Normans decided to absorb it into England. Robert d'Umfraville, from a Normandy family, was granted the barony of Prudhoe and a massive rampart of stone and clay, and a tower, rose on the castle site.

The castle was totally remodelled, with a curtain wall, as the Scots kept up

their attacks in the early 12th Century.

There is a link between Aydon and Prudhoe. One of the Aydon owners, Walter Fitz Gilbert, married Emma d'Umfraville, whose father and brothers were barons at Prudhoe.

When the male line of the d'Umfravilles came to an end, the barony came into the possession of the Percy family through marriage in 1398.

Prudhoe Castle is still owned by the Duke of Northumberland. The castle came into the guardianship of the Ministry of Works in 1966 – the same year as Aydon Castle – and is now managed by English Heritage.

Aydon Castle interior

At least 25 of the 120 acres at Aydon were let - but that brought in only 14s 7d, or 73p, a year.

Robert's son also served in the Scottish wars, but the family luck did not improve when the Scots King David invaded in 1346 and Aydon once again surrendered.

The family finally called it a day in Northumberland in the early 17th Century.

Future occupants did not have much money to spend on Aydon and that, together with its out-of-the-way location, meant it survived relatively unaltered to become today one of the finest examples of a 13th Century manor house in England.

The next owners of Aydon, the Carnabys of Hexham, didn't fare much better.

Ralph Carnaby paid heavily for being a royalist colonel in the Civil War and Aydon was sold for £653 in 1654 to William Collinson, a Parliamentary captain stationed at Tynemouth Castle. Aydon Castle was then bought by Newcastle town clerk William Douglas, whose grand-daughter Anne married Edward Blackett.

The castle became a farmhouse and in 1966 was entrusted by the Blackett family to the Ministry of Works, which carried out the first major repairs for 400 years. With so many ups and downs, its walls have a story to tell.

English Heritage visitor operations manager Stephen Farthing says: "The description of 'hidden gem' is often used, but Aydon Castle certainly is that. You feel as if you are stepping into a different world."

Restoration work has involved clearing partitions and floors inserted in the 18th and 19th Centuries to increase sleeping accommodation. This has returned the castle hall to what would have greeted a 14th Century visitor.

But the most atmospheric space is the kitchen wing, with its stone sink, stone cupboards and ranks of square holes at the tops of two walls for nesting doves or pigeons - fresh eggs and meat on tap!

Visitors can, in these tranquil times, enjoy a stroll around the outer walls, parts of which skirt the drop above the Cor Burn. At the prettiest spot on the walk, look up and you will see the stone latrine chutes directly above.

Which means that in medieval times, the view was not the most pressing consideration for those who lived in Aydon Castle.

Remains at Corbridge Roman site

Corbridge Roman site, run by English Heritage, is half a mile north-west of Corbridge. Tel: (01434) 652220.

Open April 1 to September 30, 10am-6pm daily. October 1 to 31, 10am to 4pm daily. November 1 to March 31, 10am to 4pm Saturday and Sunday.

Aydon Castle is a mile and a half north-east of Corbridge on a minor road signposted off the A68 or B6321. Open April 1 to September 30, 10am to 6pm daily. Tel: (01434) 632450.

Prudhoe Castle is on a minor road off the A695.

Open April 1 to September 30, 10am-6pm daily.

Tel: (01661) 833459.

Birdoswald Roman Fort

There are views in the North of England which royally repay every ounce of effort expended to reach them and, once seen, stay in the mind's eye.

One such is the vista from the Cumbrian side of the River Irthing, which separates the county from Northumberland.

It is from a high spur on the south west corner of Birdoswald Roman fort. The land plunges sharply into the partly-wooded gorge of the meandering river.

It is a giddying aspect, and one which was described by a 19th Century Earl of Carlisle as being akin to the view from Troy.

It has long been a special place, for a prehistoric stone-lined burial chamber was discovered there.

You don't exactly have to hurry to appreciate the view before it is gone, but the expert consensus is that go it will. Excavations at Birdoswald have shown that the drop was once many feet further away and that eventually the spur will erode and the fort will plunge into the river.

For 300 years, Birdoswald, on the edge of the village of Gilsland, was one of the forts which were part of the Hadrian's Wall frontier system. It has a long history of occupation, from the Roman to the Dark Ages of the Fifth and Sixth Centuries, and from medieval to modern times.

In fact, Birdoswald was farmed until the 1980s. There was no mains water and supplies were drawn from the River Irthing, while the farm was not connected to the electricity grid until 40 years ago. That chimes in with the feeling that the modern world has, until recently, passed Birdoswald by and that the echoes of the past are still loud and clear.

A gateway to Birdoswald Fort

After the Dark Ages occupation, Birdoswald goes silent until the 13th Century.

The records suggest that Radulpho de Birdoswald had a house on the site.

Robert the Bruce attacked Gilsland in 1311 and this was followed by raids in 1333 and 1345.

There are the remains of a tower house built between 1200-1500 and there is evidence that the Roman West Gate was still being used, 1,000 years after it was constructed.

A bastle, or fortified farmhouse, was built on the site of the tower house in the late 16th Century when the tenants were the Tweddle family.

They did not have an easy time of it in what was reiving country.

In 1588 Robert Tweddle complained that the "Elliots" had stolen 30 cattle, horses and household goods.

The Nixons also raided, as did the Armstrongs, who took 40 cattle and 40 sheep.

In the late 17th Century the bastle was replaced by another building, part of which survives in the present farmhouse, which is now used as accommodation for visitors.

Anthony and Margaret Bowman built the main part of the house in 1745.

Henry Norman bought Birdoswald in the 1840s and in 1858 added the tower and porch which can be seen today.

He hired the Potter brothers from Newcastle to excavate

the east and south gates of the fort.

His son, Oswald, auctioned off the estate and sold Henry's collection of Roman sculptures and inscriptions which are now at Tullie House Museum in Carlisle.

The estate was sold in the 1970s to Lord Henley and in 1984 it was acquired by Cumbria County Council.

English Heritage began excavations in 1987 and has now taken over the management of the site.

In this rugged country, it paid to make use of any resources to hand and all the farm buildings were constructed with stone taken from the fort.

Built into one wall is part of an altar dedicated to the troops who manned the fort in the Third and Fourth Centuries. They represent the region's unlikely link with Romania.

In the First and early Second Centuries, the Dacians, from what is now Romania, were the tough enemies of Rome under their king Decebalus.

Eventually, the Emperor Trajan triumphed over the Dacians, whose fighting qualities impressed the Romans so much that they were recruited as auxiliary soldiers.

A cohort of Dacians worked on the building of Hadrian's Wall and Birdoswald became the home of what was known as the First Cohort of Dacians, Hadrian's Own, consisting of 1,000 infantry.

Although they were at Birdoswald for 200 years, they never forgot their roots, with the Dacian curved sword being carved on building inscriptions.

A gravestone from Birdoswald is for a child called Decebalus, after the Dacian king.

The cemetery at the fort was discovered 44 years ago when ploughing turned up pots containing cremated bone.

One gravestone is that of Aurelius Concordius, the infant son of the commander of the Dacian garrison, Aurelius Julianus, whose name appears on tablets marking the building of granaries at the fort.

Inscriptions record the names of 17 top officers, including the commander from the 230s Flavius Maximianus, who was a former member of the Praetorian Guard.

Another tombstone commemorates a soldier called Septimus, aged 40, who served for 18 years with the Dacian cohort.

The Wall was a pretty cosmopolitan place. One gravestone is to G Cossurtius Saturninus, of the Legion VI Victrix, who was born in North Africa.

In the fort cemetery area, a Third Century cooking pot containing created remains was found, and an accompanying drinking cup from Gaul.

The funeral stones are not the only ones to tell a story. On show in the fort's exhibition is an altar dedicated to Silvanus, the god of woodland and uncultivated land, by the Venatores Bannienses, which means the "hunters of Banna" – the Roman name for Birdoswald.

A scratched name on a piece of pottery is that of Martinus, a cavalry troop commander from a unit based at the fort in the time of Hadrian.

Banna is also recorded on the Rudge Cup, a bronze bowl unearthed in Wiltshire which carries the names of forts along Hadrian's Wall.

The soldiers at Birdoswald would have lived 10 to a room in barracks of eight rooms, which have been located under the farm buildings and adjacent courtyard.

It has been discovered that in the Third Century, one barrack was remodelled to include officers' quarters with underfloor heating.

The only drill and exercise hall to be found in any auxiliary fort in the Roman Empire has been identified at Birdoswald.

It was 48 metres long and 16 metres wide, and

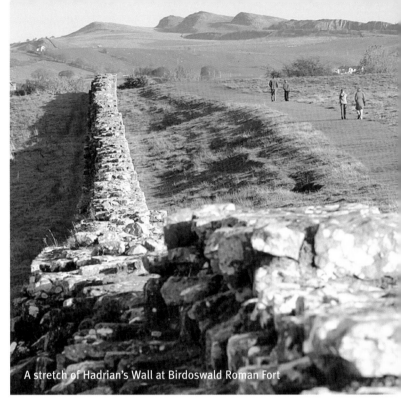
A stretch of Hadrian's Wall at Birdoswald Roman Fort

provided the troops with an all-weather facility.

The drill hall remains may be the "church" which was referred to by the intrepid schoolmaster Reginald Bainbrigg, from Appleby in Cumbria, who visited Birdoswald in 1599.

He wrote: "I came to Birdoswald, whiche doth seame to have bene some great towne by the great ruynes thereof."

The fort has also given up some fascinating finds.

In the 19th Century, diggers discovered a gilt-bronze statue of Hercules, thought to have been made in the image of the Emperor Commodus.

A stone statue of the goddess Fortuna was found in the bath house of the commander's house in 1855. The first fragments ever found of a leather Roman army tent were discovered at Birdoswald in the 1930s.

And pity the poor individual who lost a bronze purse full of silver coins which was found in the rampart at the side of the fort.

Birdoswald is open from March 1-November 9 from 10am-5.30pm. During the winter months the exterior only is open.

There is a tea shop.

Telephone (01697) 747602.

The fort is reached off the A69 via Greenhead and Gilsland.

Gilsland

On a bend in a dramatic river gorge stands what can only be described as a celebrity stone.

Left: River Irthing

Above: The Popping Stone, Irthing Valley

It's called the Popping Stone and can be found on the banks of the River Irthing on the boundary between Northumberland and Cumbria.

The ensemble of one, large, rounded and two smaller sandstone boulders is yet another example of the surprises which are hidden away in the quiet corners of this most diverse of regions.

The stone is reputed to be where the young lawyer Walter Scott – later the novelist Sir Walter – proposed to his bride-to-be, Charlotte Carpenter, in 1797.

Scott had met Charlotte at a dance in Gilsland's Shaws Hotel, next to the gorge, at a time when the village was drawing visitors because of its growing reputation as a spa resort.

Charlotte was described as being "without the features of a regular beauty", but she was "rich in personal attributes, a complexion of the clearest and lightest olive, eyes large, deep set and dazzling, of the finest Italian brown, and a profusion of silken tresses, black as the raven's wing."

The walk along the riverbank of the wooded gorge, complete with waterfall, is a delight.

But, according to Gilsland historian and archaeology graduate Will Higgs, that may not have been the reason Walter took

Charlotte to the stone.

The stone, believes Will, has an ancient pedigree and Scott, who was fascinated by folklore and legend, would have been attracted to such a site.

Will says: "Why does he take the trouble to march Miss Carpenter all the way to the Popping Stone if it wasn't already locally famous, or more likely infamous, as a rendezvous for lovers?"

It is Will's theory that the stone may have been the centre of myth and ritual connected to fertility and wooing.

What appear to be peck marks, possibly caused by chipping, are apparent on the rounded top of the main boulder.

Hearsay has it that women would chip or scrape off bits of the sandstone to

Gilsland Spa Hotel

The Gilsland Spa Hotel sits 700ft above sea level – a reminder of the village's heady days as a spa resort.

From the turn of the last century, it was used as a convalescent home for Co-operative Society members in the North of England but it also welcomed paying visitors as well as the patients.

Today, the Co-op Group owns 95% of the shares in the hotel, with the rest spread among Co-op societies.

The hotel, along with others in the area, catered for the visitors who arrived to partake of the sulphur water and chalybeate, or iron springs. The waters were said to cure rheumatism, kidney disease, indigestion, low spirits, gout, consumption, skin complaints and "worn out constitutions". As well as drinking the water, visitors could have hot and cold sulphur baths.

In its 19th Century heyday, bathing rooms, refreshment and book stalls lined the banks of the River Irthing.

But in the 17th and much of the 18th Centuries, Gilsland had been a dangerous place to visit. Of particular note was Mumps Hall, an inn with a landlady, Meg O'Mumps, who, along with her husband and regulars, was said to have specialised in relieving travellers of their worldly goods.

The inn, now a house, features in Sir Walter Scott's novel Guy Mannering.

Towards the end of the 18th Century, people, including Walter Scott and the poet Robbie Burns, began calling to take the waters.

Shaws Hotel was one of the establishments built to cater for the trade, which increased with the arrival of a railway station as part of the 1836 Newcastle-Carlisle railway.

The building was destroyed by fire in 1859 and what is now the Gilsland Spa Hotel replaced it.

Jim Lamb, former director of the Newcastle Co-op, a director of the North Eastern Co-op board and chairman for nine years of Gilsland Spa board, has researched the history of the hotel. He found that in 1893 it was leased to the Gilsland Spa and Hydro company of South Shields.

>

There were three classes of guest, all with separate dining rooms.

Third-class breakfast time was 8am, second-class 8.30am while first-class could have a lie-in until 9am. The niceties of class continued with third and second-class guests having their main meal in the middle of the day. First-class had luncheon at midday and dinner in the early evening.

The Gilsland Convalescent Hotel Souvenir of 1903 did not hold back in its description of the area.

"Gilsland is God's Country. So multifarious are its charms, one is inclined to think, not to be profane, that the Almighty in some primeval period, rested on the spot and left the impress of the Celestial upon the Terrestrial.

"There the invalid can breathe the life-giving air which will brighten the faded lustre of his eye and restore the emaciated frame."

Under the Co-op, the daily routine began with a warning bell at 8am and porridge and milk, ham and eggs at 8.30am.

Dinner was at 12.30pm with roast beef, vegetables and pudding, then tea at 4.30pm of bread, butter and jam, an 8pm supper of bread and butter, and lights out at 10.30pm.

When it came to baths, guests were spoilt for choice. There were hot and cold plunge baths, sulphur water baths, Russian and Turkish baths, and vapour and needle baths.

In the days before heated bedrooms, the guests queued at 9.30pm at a hatch to have hot water bottles filled.

In the 1930s the rules stipulated that patients were forbidden to use their bedrooms between 10am-7pm and, if they felt ill, they were not allowed to go to bed without permission of the matron.

A notice in the hotel dance hall also read: "Male residents are requested not to molest or interfere with the maids in the course of their duties."

The hotel was taken over at the outbreak of the Second World War by Newcastle Corporation, to be used as a maternity home away from the threat of bombing. More than 1,000 North-Easterners were born at the hotel.

In the 1950s, a working holiday scheme offered Co-op guild volunteers free room, food and travelling expenses in return for their services in the hotel.

Jim Lamb reckons that the last convalescents used the hotel in the early 1980s.

He says: "While they talked about the waters, it is my view that it was the bracing, clean country air which was of benefit to the convalescents."

The building is now run as a country hotel.

wear in bags around their neck to ensure fertility, or put fragments under their pillow to dream of their future husband. Will believes the Walter Scott link with the Popping Stone was promoted in Victorian times for the benefit of the Gilsland spa visitor trade.

"But the Popping Stone goes back a long way before the Victorian period as a fertility source," he says.

"I don't think it was called the Popping Stone because Scott proposed there. The traditions associated with the Popping Stone may be evidence for its importance in the past.

"I suggest that it is an unusual type of megalithic monument and should be officially recognised as a potential ancient site."

Near the stone there was also a Hawthorn, known as the Kissing Bush, which is now gone.

As Victorian photographs and early 20th Century postcards show, the stone drew many visitors, including photographers.

"Many of the photographs are of couples and young women on the stone," says Will.

It also appears that the stone changed shape in the 1870s. This has been put down to people chipping pieces off but Will thinks the appearance of the stone could have been altered to avoid offending the polite sensibilities of Victorian visitors.

Whatever, the stone is not the only surprise in the 140-acre estate belonging to the Gilsland Spa Hotel which sits on the crest of the gorge.

At the head of the gorge is the Crammel Linn waterfall.

From the corner of the hotel car park, the visitor takes a footpath to descend to the river where, beside a footbridge, flows a sulphur spring encased in a man-made stone frame.

This is one of the springs which put Gilsland on the map as a spa.

A short walk along the riverbank is a sight which has an eerie touch.

Amid encroaching woodland is an outdoor swimming pool. It was once used by guests of the hotel but was abandoned in 1939.

Saplings are now growing out of the pool, where porcelain linings are still visible, and the moss-covered steps descend into what is now only a blanket of vegetation.

At what would once have been a riverside place of happy and noisy times, there is now only the rustling of the leaves.

Footbridge over the River Irthing at Gilsland

The Directory of Cumberland and Westmorland in 1829 paints a lyrical picture of the delights awaiting the visitor to Gilsland:

It was a village with very large and elegantly-furnished inns in an area "highly celebrated for its sulphureted and chalybeate spas which are situated in the romantic and picturesque vale of the Irthing.

"The men of science may botanize or ransack the mineral productivity of a wild and mountainous domain. Antiquarians may explore the numerous remains."

Hotels catered for three different classes of visitors "who will mix in the assembly rooms where rank has no influence in the choice of partners for the dance."

There were billiard tables, libraries, newsrooms, music and plenty of trout for the angler and game for the sportsman "so that ennui can seldom find a place amongst the gay and numerous visitors who throng Gilsland during the summer season."

The waters were analysed by Dr William Reid Clanny of Sunderland who found that the sulphur water contained hydrogen and carbonic acid gas, salt, carbonate of soda and lime, and silica.

The iron spring water was made up of sulphate of iron and lime, and carbonate of magnesia and silica.

He wrote that the sulphur water was a "highly esteemed cure for scrofulous habits and a valuable remedy for atomic gout".

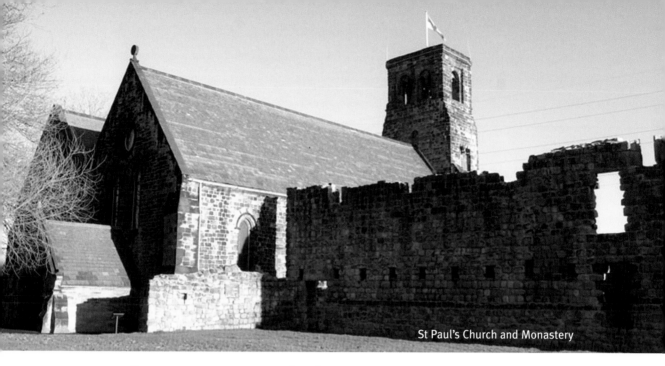

St Paul's Church and Monastery

Bede's World

The depth of the well of talent which has always characterised the North-East is illustrated by the long line of great sons and daughters which the region has produced.

Inventors, military leaders, industrial pioneers, musicians, writers, sportsmen and women, churchmen, politicians – the list goes on. But who is the greatest of them all?

A strong candidate is a monk who spent most of his life on the banks of the Tyne 1,300 years ago.

The Venerable Bede, born in 673, served the dual monastery of Wearmouth-Jarrow.

He entered the monastery at the age of seven and spent two years at St

Peter's monastery at Wearmouth and then moved to St Paul's monastery in Jarrow.

Bede became arguably the greatest scholar in 8th Century Europe, and he is still published and read today. His great work, *The Ecclesiastical History of the English People*, covered 800 years over five volumes and was finished in 731.

It earned him the accolade of being England's first historian.

At a time when most

writing was a recording of fact, Bede created the concept of writing history and the idea of a unified England centuries before it happened.

He also produced scores of books discussing theology, astronomy, natural science, poetry, grammar, mathematics and chronology, and popularised the BC/AD dating system and the calculation of the date of Easter.

Bede made the North-East the centre of European learning. The scriptorium at Jarrow, where books were copied by hand, could not keep up with the demand for Bede's works from across Europe.

The enormity of Bede's achievements can – and should – be grasped by visiting Bede's World in

A historical re-enactor at the site

Anglo-Saxon farm

Jarrow, Tyne and Wear, where a new museum is devoted to his life and times.

It overlooks the site of Bede's monastery and St Paul's Church with its Saxon chancel above which is the original dedication stone from April 23, 685 – the earliest surviving in any English church.

Bede would probably have been present when the stone was laid.

In 1899 Bede was confirmed by the Pope as a saint and a doctor of the Church – the only Englishman to be honoured with the title.

It is little wonder that preparations are advanced to have the Wearmouth-Jarrow monastery site declared the North-East's third world heritage site.

Bede's World curator Laura Sole, who studied Anglo-

That Bede was able to flourish was very much due to a Northumbrian nobleman called Benedict Biscop, who was born around 628.

At the age of 25 he decided to travel to Rome. In all he visited Rome six times and also gained inspiration from 17 monasteries along the way.

On his return to Northumbria, King Ecgfrith gave him land at the mouth of the Wear to found St Peter's monastery.

A similar gift led to the setting up of St Paul's monastery at Jarrow.

From his visits to Rome Benedict Biscop collected books, relics, vessels, vestments and religious pictures for Wearmouth-Jarrow.

Three great bibles were produced at Jarrow in Bede's lifetime. One, the Codex Amiatinus, covers 2,060 pages and used the skins of 515 animals.

A copy is on show at the Bede's World museum.

The first abbot of Jarrow, Ceolfrith, set off for Rome with the bible to present it to the Pope but died in France.

The Jarrow bible is now in Florence. It is the oldest single-volume bible in the world.

The chancel of today's St Paul's Church was originally a separate small Anglo-Saxon church.

The central Anglo-Saxon window space in the south wall of the chancel contains a circular window made from Anglo-Saxon coloured glass which was found during the excavations of the monastery site.

Another relic in the church is what for years was known as Bede's chair but radiocarbon dating has put it at between the 9th and 11th Centuries.

It is believed that the monastery was raided in 794 by the Vikings. By 1074 it had been re-founded.

The remains are now in the guardianship of English Heritage and are managed by Bede's World.

in 1985 the clearance of 20 huge oil storage tanks from the adjacent Shell-Mex site allowed the creation of an 11-acre Anglo-Saxon farm.

In 2000 the Queen officially opened the new museum complex – the latest piece in the £9m Bede's World jigsaw.

It houses some of the finds from excavations of the monastery site in the 1960s and 70s which were led by Durham University's Professor Rosemary Cramp.

The digs unearthed pieces of what is thought to be the oldest coloured window glass in Europe, with around 1,000 fragments being discovered.

"To find so many was incredible," says Laura.

Some of the best pieces were made into new windows, based on 7th and 8th Century designs, which are on display in the museum and the church.

The international contacts which the monastery enjoyed are suggested by finds such as a tiny elephant-ivory box and the remains of fine red beakers, probably made in the Near East.

Also excavated were rods made from coloured glass from which slices could be taken to ornament fine items such as book covers or crosses for the altar.

Bede's World evolved from Jarrow Hall, which is now part of the site and looks over St Paul's Church.

The listed hall was the home of the Bede Monastery Museum from 1974 and now houses the Bede's World café/restaurant.

But the hall, built around 1785, was threatened with demolition at the start of the 1970s. It had fallen into dereliction after having been used by the then Jarrow Council as a storage depot.

With its fate in the balance, the hall was given to the St Paul's Development Trust, which carried out a £50,000 restoration.

The hall was built by Simon Temple, who was born in 1759 in Westoe Village, South Shields, into a shipbuilding family.

He invested in coal mining in the shape of the Alfred pit in Jarrow and opened a shipyard in the town which built six frigates and two sloops for the Navy.

But bankruptcy followed after he bought Hylton Castle in Sunderland and a hefty investment failed in a mine at South Shields.

The hall passed through several hands and was let to the Shell-Mex company in 1920, before passing to Jarrow Council in 1935.

Saxon, Norse and Celtic at Cambridge University, says: "Bede was called the Teacher of the Middle Ages. Europe clamoured for copies of his work.

"As soon as the printing press was invented, copies of his works were produced across Europe and he has never gone out of print.

"He laid the ground of European knowledge. He was the first Englishman to use the term 'English' and the writing of his history was an incredible task, a tremendous undertaking.

"He was a genius who was able to absorb every subject."

It has taken an age for a suitable centre highlighting Bede's work to be set up near the St Paul's monastery site in South Tyneside. A small museum opened in 1974 in Georgian Jarrow Hall and

Profound though Bede's achievements were, it was thought to be important that visitors to the Jarrow site should also be given a taste of what everyday life was like at the monastery.

The Anglo-Saxon farm on the Bede's World site is called Gyrwe (pronounced Yeerweh) from the Old English name for Jarrow.

The farm is a long-term experimental project to re-create the landscape into which Bede was born.

Gyrwe has been based on archaeological evidence, contemporary documents and manuscript illustrations.

The farm grows crops of the time, pond reeds for thatching, uses hazel and willow for fencing, flax for oil and linen and has a herb garden.

Animals include old sheep breeds such as Hebridean, Ronaldsay, Manx Loghtan and Soay, while the oxen are Dexters, which are the size and shape of Anglo-Saxon cattle.

The pigs are a cross between wild boar and old Tamworth and Berkshire breeds. Evidence from the excavation of an Anglo-Saxon site at Thirlings in Northumberland has informed the reconstruction of a hall.

A dig at the early monastery at Hartlepool provided the basis for the re-creation of a monk's cell.

Another replica is a type of Anglo-Saxon wooden tent-like structure above a pit, from excavations in Northumberland, and which is thought to have been a grain store or workshop.

The River Don, a tributary of the Tyne, runs beside Bede's World and its mudflats are managed for birds such as redshank and lapwing.

Bede's treasures bequeathed at his death included grains of incense and pepper.

Traces of a building with high status flooring and painted plaster walls were found and it is believed to have accommodated visits from Northumbrian kings.

Bede's World seeks to raise awareness about this multi-talented man and has a massive education programme which sees 25,000 schoolchildren visiting every year.

Bede died on May 25, 735, at the age of 63.

He was buried at the church in Jarrow but in the 11th Century his bones were taken to Durham Cathedral where his tomb is today.

It was Notker Balbulus, a 9th Century monk and biographer of Charlemagne who wrote: "God.... Who on the fourth day of creation brought forth the sun in the east, ordained in the sixth age of mankind Bede as a new sun in the west to illuminate the whole globe."

Bede's World on Church Bank in Jarrow is two minutes from the A19 Tyne Tunnel south entrance and a short walk from Bede Metro station.

Tel: (0191) 489-2106.

Opening times are April-October 10am-5.30pm, Sundays noon-5.30pm.

November-March closing time is 4.30pm.

St Paul's church is normally open 10am-4pm Monday-Saturday and 2.30pm-4pm on Sundays.

Looking over Redesdale from Bremenium Roman Fort at High Rochester

Bremenium Roman Fort

If Hadrian's Wall was the eventual northernmost frontier of Roman expansion, then the fort of Bremenium was on the edge of the empire.

For more than 200 years, the fort, now the hamlet of High Rochester in Northumberland National Park, was the most northerly occupied base in the entire Roman empire.

It was a dicey place to be, as indicated by the fact that the garrison was provided with a giant catapult which fired heavy stone balls.

Two of the projectiles can be seen mounted on the corners of the porch of the former schoolhouse in the village of Rochester below the fort, which is built mainly from Roman stone.

After a short climb to Bremenium, visitors can wander around its perimeter walls to gain a sense of how wild this posting must have been, and how it retains an air of remoteness today.

The base is one of the fascinating features of Redesdale.

The valley of the River Rede is 37 miles long. The river rises on the slopes of Carter Fell on the Northumberland-Scotland border and eventually joins the North Tyne near Bellingham.

Bremenium means the Place of the Roaring Stream - a reference to the Sills Burn, whose deep and narrow valley threads through the landscape near the fort. After prolonged heavy rain or a thaw, the Sills Burn can indeed make itself heard. At other times, it makes a

One of the figures to emerge from Bremenium's past is Julia Lucilla.

She is known from having commissioned a tombstone to her husband Rufinus, who was the fort commander. The stone is in the church at nearby Elsdon.

"It reads like a CV. She is obviously tremendously proud of him and lists all his army and civilian posts," says Roman expert Lindsay Allason-Jones.

Rufinus had been sub-curator of the Flaminian Way, which was a famous road through Rome, while Julia refers to herself as a senator's daughter.

"So here we have a woman from the top echelons of Roman society," says Lindsay.

"Her husband is assigned to his position at High Rochester in Northumberland and there is not a soul of her status there.

"She must have been a bit like the colonel's wife at a fort in Indian country in the Wild West. She must also have been bored out of her mind and wondering what she had let herself in for.

"She is in enemy territory and the nearest other senator's daughter would probably have been in York."

At the Fulling Mill Museum in Durham, there are more clues to Julia's life.

An altar was dedicated to Rufinus and Julia by Eutychus, who describes himself as their "freed man."

This is a Greek name.

Lindsay says: "It looks like he was the couple's slave and moved with them to High Rochester with his family.

"The fort still feels a little remote even now and would have felt incredibly remote to Julia.

"But she seems to have been so proud of her husband that she would probably have wanted to be with him wherever he went."

Gateway feature at Bremenium Roman fort

pretty picture with twin waterfalls and primrose-covered banks.

The fort occupies a strong position on a low hill with views over Upper Redesdale and beyond. Recent research suggests that it was built on top of a previous native settlement – possibly a prestige Iron Age centre.

Remarkably, the site is included on Ptolemy's map of the ancient world, compiled in Alexandria in the Second Century, which perhaps indicates its importance as a pre-Roman centre.

The fort site was chosen by Julius Agricola, Roman Governor of Britain, in the late First Century as part of the thrust into Scotland. Bremenium became an outpost fort beyond Hadrian's Wall – a sort of early warning station.

Today, there are houses inside the fort walls, including two 16th Century bastles, or fortified farmhouses.

Where the fort buildings stood is now known as the village green.

One of the fort's roles was to keep a wary eye on and gather intelligence about the tribes to the north of Hadrian's Wall.

It was also a staging post and guard base on the major military highway, called Dere Street, built by Agricola to carry the campaign into Scotland.

Up to 500 men were shoe-horned into Bremenium. The earliest known garrison was a mixed

A replica carving of a warrior god at Brigantium

A roundhouse at Brigantium

Visitors can take a walk through 10,000 years of Redesdale history at the Brigantium archaeological reconstruction site in Rochester.

The centre has been created by Lord Redesdale, who studied archaeology at Newcastle University.

An Iron Age roundhouse has been built, based on a settlement excavated at nearby Woolaw.

That consisted of four stone-built roundhouses in a rectangular area enclosed by a stone wall.

The Brigantium structure is currently the only stone-built roundhouse in Britain.

A mixture of clay, straw and water was used to make wattle for the inside wall, which is draught-proof and also reflects the heat from the central hearth.

A rocky outcrop on the site has been used to demonstrate a hunter-gatherer rock shelter and also a rock cavity shrine which was found at nearby Yardhope on the Otterburn military range.

An image of a warrior god, holding a spear and shield, which was carved into the rock at Yardhope, has been replicated.

The site also includes re-constructions of an early Bronze Age burial cairn, excavated at Dour Hill in the area, cup and ring carvings, a four-poster stone circle, Roman graves, a section of cobbled Roman road, and a dowsing trail.

infantry and cavalry regiment from about AD140, with the same sort of outfit in the Third Century.

Troops known from inscriptions were raised in France, Spain and Belgium.

An inscription also refers to the Bremenium Scouts, or Exploratores Bremenienses, who patrolled the surrounding lands. The role of this unit is likened by Lindsay Allason-Jones to that of Indian scouts working for the cavalry in the American West.

Lindsay, director of archaeological museums at Newcastle University, says: "Most of the time, Bremenium was in barbarian territory.

"It also minded the army's back as the troops went up Dere Street."

Unlike other forts, where civilian settlements grew up outside the walls, there seems to have been little or nothing of this nature at Bremenium.

Even the bath house was inside the fort.

"It was always a dangerous place. It would have been fraught with hazards," says Lindsay.

"It was still a dodgy place up to the 18th Century." Hence the bastle houses.

Above: The stone carving from Bremenium of Venus washing her hair

In 1581, the Rochester villagers lodged a complaint with Elizabeth I's commissioners against the Elliots of Liddesdale, who had raided on several occasions, taking livestock and household goods "so that the town was laid waste for five years".

Lindsay says: "The Redesdale baddies were all over the place.

"People were looking for somewhere defensible and the fort walls offered some protection."

Something of a siege mentality may be guessed from the fact that two double granaries in the fort could store large stocks of grain in times of emergencies or to supply units operating north of the Wall.

Multiple ramparts

protected the fort, which could have accommodated up to 16 barracks tightly packed into a total fort area of just under five acres.

Although an outpost, the fort has yielded finds such as an altar to Minerva, an underfloor heating system, spring-fed baths and a stone panel carved with images of Venus washing her hair while attended by two nymphs.

The carving may have been used for the front of a water tank and was based on a Third Century BC Greek original.

"It was a famous depiction and would have been well-known in Rome.

"It looks like the person who carved it at Bremenium was told what to do and had never seen the original," says Lindsay.

"As a result, the ladies who are depicted have a very Celtic look.

"It was a frontier fort but they have gone to the trouble of carving this in classical style.

"Although it was a very dangerous place, they felt it was worth decorating."

Brigantium is on the A68 at Rochester, north of Otterburn.
There is a café and the site is open until around 5pm daily.
Telephone (01830) 520-801.
Bremenium is a short walk over fields from Brigantium.
It can also be reached by car via the minor road which leaves the A68 on the edge of Rochester village.

The mound at Elsdon where the castle once stood

Elsdon and Otterburn

The village of Elsdon sits in a natural bowl surrounded by hills.

That bowl contains as much history as you could wish for and, while the village is only 30 miles or so from Newcastle, it is a world away from city life.

The village is held to be the most complete example of a medieval settlement in Northumberland National Park.

Its main landmark is the 14th Century Elsdon Tower, built with 8ft-thick walls within which a spiral staircase winds to the parapets. The outer walls sport crests and shields of the families associated with the tower - the Percys and the Umfravilles.

The Norman Robert de Umfraville, a relative of William the Conqueror, had been granted the Lordship of Redesdale, following which a timber castle was built at Elsdon.

The raised platform on which the fortress stood - the finest earthwork castle in Northumberland - is known as the Mote Hills which rise above the Elsdon Burn to the north of the village.

Elsdon Tower is recorded in 1415 as a vicar's pele

and was certainly built for security.

After 560 years as a rectory, the tower passed into private ownership in 1961. One inhabitant was the Rev Charles Dodgson, great grandfather of *Alice in Wonderland* author Lewis Carroll and who left a vivid account in 1762 of what it was like to live there.

He wrote: "The vestibule of the castle is a low stable and above it is the kitchen, in which there are two little beds, joining each other. The curate and his wife lay in one and

Percy Cross

The hundreds of men who lie in mass graves in Elsdon churchyard are likely to be those who met their end by moonlight on August 19, 1388, in the Battle of Otterburn.

Today, amid a group of trees off the main road through the village of Otterburn, the Percy Cross stands as a monument to the battle.

It came about after the Scots, under Sir Archibald Douglas, attacked Carlisle while James, Earl of Douglas, led another force in a raid as far as Newcastle.

During skirmishes outside Newcastle, Douglas snatched the lance pennon of his opposite number Sir Henry Percy – Shakespeare's Hotspur.

This was a slight too far and, after Douglas headed back to Scotland with his booty, Hotspur and his men pursued them by means of a forced march from Newcastle.

The Scots were camped overnight at Otterburn. When Hotspur arrived, he threw his tired men straight into battle. This meant the English lost the advantage of being able to use their longbows.

The battle, whose story is told in the Chevy Chase ballad, saw fierce hand-to-hand fighting. It ended in victory for the Scots. Hotspur was captured and led away for ransom.

But Douglas was killed and his body was taken to Melrose Abbey. Hotspur later had his revenge on the Douglas clan in the Battle of Homildon Hill.

The cross was erected in the 18th Century to replace an earlier battle stone. A lintel from Otterburn Tower was used. Two pieces of iron at the base are what is left of hooks from which cooking pots were hung.

Otterburn Tower dates from medieval times. The tower site was re-built as a castellated mansion in 1830 for Thomas James of Tynedale and is now a country house hotel.

The Battle of Otterburn and Chevy Chase echoed over the years. Otterburn Hall, also a hotel, is said to have been built in 1870 for Lord James Douglas who received the land in recompense for the death in battle of an ancestor.

The building of a toll road through Otterburn made the Percy Arms Inn a stop for the Chevy Chase coach running from Newcastle to Edinburgh and the Blucher, on the Newcastle-Jedburgh trip.

Margery the maid in the other.

"I lay in the parlour between two beds to keep me from being frozen to death. The winds enter from every quarter and are apt to creep into bed with one.

"My head is entrenched in three nightcaps and my throat is fortified with a pair of stockings twisted in the form of a cravat. As washing is very cheap I wear two shirts at a time and for want of a wardrobe hang my great coat on my back."

Freezing maybe, but those in the tower were lucky they were behind defensive walls. In 1554 villagers complained to what officialdom could be found that 400 men of the Elliot and Armstrong clans had staged a raid in which 14 people were killed and 200 cattle and £500 in money and goods were stolen. Witness to all of this was the village's medieval church, parts of which date from the 12th Century and which is dedicated to St Cuthbert whose body is said to have rested at the site a short time during the wanderings of the Lindisfarne monks.

The village of Elsdon with Elsdon Tower (top) and St Cuthbert's Church in the middle.

The skulls of three horses were found inside the spire in 1877 during restoration work. One theory is that this could have been a continuation of a pre-Christian practice. But in 1810 a far more dramatic discovery took place, when the removal of earth mounds against the nave's north wall revealed the bones of more than 100 individuals in double rows with, as records say, "the skulls of one row within the thigh bones of the other, packed into the smallest possible compass." During the 1877 works, a large number of skeletons were unearthed under the north wall.

"From the manner in which they were packed it is inferred that they had been buried at one time and shortly before the erection of the nave, since the foundations of the north wall were found to be not so deeply laid as other parts of the church, the builders evidently wishing to avoid disturbing the bodies."

As this building work had taken place around 1400, it is believed the bodies were of those who lost their lives in the nearby Battle of Otterburn in 1388.

A likely link with the Battle of Otterburn was the discovery in 1987 of a late 14th Century sword on the Army's Otterburn Training Range.

The weapon was found during the clearance of old shells from ground at Silloans before new drains were laid.

The sword was 18 inches below ground and had a tempered steel blade, an iron pommel which once held a jewel and fragments of a leather scabbard.

It was a quality weapon which would not have been needlessly discarded.

It was sent to Durham University, which identified it as belonging to the Battle of Otterburn period.

One theory is that it was taken from a high-ranking Englishman in the Otterburn defeat, but how it came to be resting in a boggy field is a mystery.

Otterburn Towers Hotel

Above: The figure of Bacchus over a former pub at Elsdon

The churchyard contains one of the most intriguing collections of old gravestones in the North-East, including images such as skull and crossbones and Adam and Eve and the Tree of Life.

As more peaceful times arrived Elsdon, clustered around its large village green, prospered as a cross-roads for the network of cattle drove roads from Scotland into England. The circular stone pinfold, where stray livestock were kept, is still on the green.

In 1858 Elsdon had four shopkeepers, three tailors, three cloggers, a shoemaker, two dressmakers, a straw hat maker, butcher, joiner and undertaker, and a cartwright. Three inns dating from the 18th Century offered refreshment to travellers.

The Bacchus, formerly the Scotch Arms, is now a house but retains the sculpture of Bacchus sitting astride a barrel over the door.

Today Elsdon is both peaceful and pleasant but as the Rev Dodgson indicated, life in the past was often hard and this is also suggested in the verse:

*"Have ye ever been to Elsdon,
The world's unfinished nook,
It lies amid the hungry hills,
And wears a frozen look."*

Otterburn found itself in the royal spotlight when Queen Alexandra visited Alnwick Castle and was presented with a travelling rug from the village textile mill.

It was a soft blue – the first woven in a plain colour. The Queen was pleased and suggested a similar rug, a quarter of the size, would be ideal for a baby's pram. For the 1926 royal birth, just such a rug was produced, or 20 rugs as that was the minimum production run.

Euan Pringle, managing director of today's Otterburn Mill, recounts how after one pram rug went to the royal family, the others were taken by Mr Fenwick for his Newcastle store: "He sold them all and asked for more."

A small textile mill had started up at Otterburn in the 18th Century. In 1821 it was taken over by William Waddell, who specialised in rugs.

It ceased production in 1976 as UK textiles hit hard times. But it still controls manufacture of its pram rugs, selling 3,500 a year.

The mill now sells clothing and there is an information centre and coffee shop. Visitors can still see the 1926 diesel engine which ran the mill and an 1880 water turbine.

Washington Old Hall

For village schoolmaster Fred Hill, the sight of an historic hall in the middle of his community edging closer by the day to demolition was a cause of nagging concern.

So he did something about it.

The fortunes of Washington Old Hall, in what is now Tyne and Wear, had declined to the extent that the building had been used as a tenement for decades.

All this was in 1932, when the hall was ruled to be unfit for habitation and was closed. As speculative builders eyed the site, Fred set up a preservation committee to save the hall.

He could not have known it would take another 23 years of struggle to raise

the funds for restoration, so that the hall could open to the public.

It did so exactly 50 years ago, and Fred's fight was eminently worth it.

For halls with medieval origins are a rare commodity in Tyne and

History graduate Sheila Arbuckle has written a book on Fred Hill and his battle to save Washington Old Hall.

Fred, who was a founder member in 1932 and secretary of the hall preservation committee, was born in Chester-le-Street in County Durham 1885 as one of a family of nine and the son of a railway guard.

He started work as a teacher in 1906, just before his 21st birthday, at Washington Colliery Infants School then served with the Royal Army Medical Corps in the First World War.

He became headmaster at Cleadon Council School and then Washington Biddick School, retiring in 1948.

For many years of his long teaching career he had to deal with the consequences of the poverty and unemployment which afflicted the families of his pupils, with youngsters absent from school for reasons such as having to scavenge for coal or having no shoes.

Fred was also a keen local historian and a member of the Newcastle Society of Antiquaries, and his determination to rescue the hall and highlight its American connections became a mission. The American celebrations in 1932 of the 200th anniversary of the birth of George Washington gave Fred the chance to raise the profile of his village and its links.

He involved local schools in the celebrations which were followed by exchanges of national flags by village and American schools, and he was rewarded with a bicentennial medal presented by the United States.

The year was doubly significant, as a closing order was served on the Old Hall, requiring the tenement dwellers who occupied it to move out.

Fred had made the acquaintance of American consul William Doty and they were brought together by their shared desire to stop the hall falling into the hands of speculative builders, which would have meant demolition.

There were years of uncertainty as negotiations and tactics revolved around the price for the hall but in 1937 the preservation committee made the purchase thanks to one of its members, Geoffrey Stirling Newall, who owned Washington Chemical Works.

He came up with £350 for the hall and £50 for essential repairs.

But the building needed considerable funds to restore it, and the Depression of the 1930s and the Second World War meant that the struggle for cash dragged on for more than 20 years.

Eventually, the hall opened to the public on September 28, 1955. Fred Hill, who had been made honorary custodian in 1950, was too ill to attend, and he died at his home on the village green six weeks later.

A year later the National Trust took over the building.

Sheila says: "I got to know a little about Fred Hill and his part in buying the hall and I felt it would be good to dig a little deeper. He had the vision to save the hall and the American connection was very strong for him.

"He would have felt it was immoral to destroy the hall and that link. He was a remarkable man. It is true that had it not been for Fred Hill, the hall would have long since been demolished."

Gardens at Washington Old Hall

Wear – and the building's links with George Washington, the first American president, mark it as extra special.

Now run by the National Trust, the hall is the centrepiece of Washington village, with President Jimmy Carter among the many Americans who have visited the ancestral home of the Washington family.

The name of Washington dates from Anglo-Saxon times, with various spellings of Wessynton, Whessingtun and Wassington.

Shortly before 1183, William de Hertburn exchanged his lands at Hartburn for the manor of Washington in a deal with Hugh de Puiset, Bishop of Durham.

William styled himself de Wessynton and built a manor house on the site of the present hall. Part of the family's 13th Century hall can be seen in the present building, which largely dates from the 17th Century.

It must have been an impressive place, as Edward I visited the village on his way back from Scotland in 1304. The family was prominent in society and Sir William de Washington fought at the Battle of Otterburn in 1388.

The American link emerges in the family's coat of arms, in use by the 14th Century, which consists of two stripes and three stars in red on a white background.

The coat of arms is carved in stone on Hylton Castle, three miles away in Sunderland.

Through marriage a branch of the family became established in Lancashire and it was from this offshoot that Col John

Above: President George Washington

Left: An exhibit at Washington Old Hall

Washington emigrated to Virginia in 1656, possibly to escape the turmoil which followed the English Civil War.

The emigrants prospered and owned the Mount Vernon estate, and it was here that George Washington was born in 1732.

He became commander in chief of the Colonial Army in the War of Independence against Britain and then the first president, giving his name to the new American capital.

Cash donations from the United States were crucial in the 22-year struggle to

Right: Staircase at the Old Hall

restore the hall with the public opening ceremony being carried out by the American Ambassador.

George has a strong presence around the building. There are framed sheets of postage stamps bearing his image, and cases of Washington memorabilia donated by Americans.

They range from 19th Century needlework portraits of George and his wife Martha and porcelain and wax representations of George, to Washington bowls and coins and souvenir plaques made from oak from the Mount Vernon estate.

Also on show is the fan presented to Martha by one of George's generals, the Marquis de Lafayette, and the silver spades used by Prime Minister James Callaghan and President Carter to plant trees on their visit in 1977.

The American Ambassador planted a tulip tree from Mount Vernon on Washington village green a year later.

It is thought that most of the walls in the hall's kitchen are medieval survivals. The Great Hall is laid out with 17th Century furniture, although the fireplace is Tudor – and came from Newburn Manor at Newcastle as a gift from Lord Gort, who was part of the preservation committee.

He also donated the hall's staircase which originally came from the White Hart Hotel in Guildford.

What would have been the private room of the Washington family, off the Great Hall, is lined with Jacobean oak panels.

Upstairs, the Liberty Room is given over to a collection of George Washington portraits and pictures of events linked to the American Revolution.

The National Trust has recently bought the adjacent Edwardian Orchard House, which is used for school educational visits and also allows access to the nuttery garden.

Rows of nut trees, surrounded by wild flowers, have been planted on what was former allotment land bought by the Friends of Washington Old Hall in 1988 to preserve open views to the south of the building.

As well as the nuttery, the grounds have specially planted trees.

There is a Damson Shropshire Prune planted following an exhibition at the hall on the life of Anne Frank and which commemorates what would have been her 75th birthday.

Washington Old Hall in Washington Village is open from March until October 30, 11am-5pm. It is closed on Thursdays, Fridays and Saturdays. There is a tea shop. Telephone (0191) 416-6879.

The Tenement Room tells the story of the hall when it was subdivided and infested by mice and cockroaches.

From the 1850s to the 1930s the hall deteriorated as it was used for tenement housing with as many as 35 people crammed into its rooms in 1891.

Outside is the Jacobean garden. In the 17th Century, the symmetrical style of such gardens and the planting of flowers and herbs in compartments to make attractive patterns was a symbol of wealth.

This was because the gardens took much maintenance by teams of workers.

Hulne Priory

Gateway at Hulne Priory

Hulne Park

In the middle of Northumberland lie 3,000 acres walled off from the outside world.

It is a landscape which was earmarked for special treatment as long as 800 years ago.

In 1224 King Henry III gifted five bucks and 10 does to help stock Alnwick parks. Eventually Hulne Park, on the edge of Alnwick, supported about 1,000 fallow deer and 1,800 oak trees.

Today Hulne Park has retained an air of serenity behind 10 miles of walls.

Its earliest features are Iron Age encampments, but within the park is a spot, on a spur overlooking the River Aln, which has links to the Crusades.

Hulne Priory represents one of the earliest, if not the first, of the English

foundations of the Carmelites, or white friars.

Hulne, in fact, is said to be one of the best preserved friaries in the country.

It is also believed to be the first house of its order founded outside the Holy Land.

The story is that hermits living on Mount Carmel, threatened by the conflict surrounding the Crusades, asked Crusader Richard Fresbourn to find them a second home.

He in turn consulted his lord, William de Vescy of Alnwick, who in 1242 gave land at Hulne for the purpose. The friars occupied Hulne until the Dissolution in 1539.

The priory remains, complete with carved

Drummer Boy's uniform in the Fusiliers Museum

stone figures of a praying monk and gate custodians, sit behind medieval walls.

A hunting lodge was added in 1486 by the Fourth Earl of Northumberland, with more embellishments in the 18th Century by Robert Adam and Capability Brown, which saw a Gothic summerhouse built.

Hulne Priory is not the only religious site in the park.

In the south east corner stands the gatehouse of Alnwick Abbey, founded in 1147.

Colin Shrimpton, Northumberland Estates archivist, says: "It is quite remarkable that two religious houses should exist within walking distance of each other."

If the inhabitants of Alnwick Abbey and Hulne Priory in Hulne Park lived largely peaceful and contemplative lives, then the contrast could not be greater with those whose exploits are the stuff of a museum a short distance away in Alnwick Castle.

The Abbott's Tower in the castle houses the Fusiliers Museum of Northumberland.

What was the 5th Foot, the Northumberland Fusiliers, the Royal Northumberland Fusiliers and now the Royal Regiment of Fusiliers has strong connections with the county and with Alnwick.

The current Duke is honorary Colonel of the 6th (Northumberland) Battalion while Hugh, the Second Duke who had fought as a general in the American War of Independence, wrote to the War Office in 1782

expressing his wishes that what was then known as the 5th Regiment of Foot should take on the name of Northumberland.

But the Northumbrian link goes back even further.

In 1674, the Dutch recruited four regiments – two English, one Scots and one Irish – to help them fight the French.

Soon after, the Northumbrian Sir John Fenwick took over the command of the Irish regiment and introduced many Northern officers so that it was redesignated as an English force.

The 5th Foot fought against the French in a combined British and German army and at the Battle of Wilhelmstahl in 1762 distinguished itself by capturing 3,000 of the enemy. One of the 5th Foot's most notable recruits was

Gardens at Hulne Priory

Phoebe Hessel, who joined up at the age of 15, disguised as a man. She died in 1821 aged 108.

The regiment took part in the American War of Independence and in the Peninsular War against Napoleon in which it became known as the Fighting Fifth.

At the Siege and Relief of Lucknow in the Indian Mutiny in 1857, what was now the 5th Northumberland Fusiliers won three VCs through Sergeant Robert Grant and Privates Peter McManus and Patrick McHale.

Often, while serving abroad, disease was a greater danger than the enemy with 62 of 137 men of the Fifth stationed at Dominica in the West Indies dying of fever.

In the Second Sudan War, when the Dervishes were defeated at the Battle of Omdurman in 1898, the Northumberland Fusiliers suffered only three wounded but lost 36 men to fever.

Two battalions of the Northumberland Fusiliers fought the Boers in South Africa where Drummer, a dog owned by Major Reay of the First Battalion, was awarded several medals for bravery.

In the First World War, the 149th Northumberland Brigade lost almost 2,000 men – virtually two-thirds of its strength – during the Second Battle of Ypres. The 16th Battalion of the Northumberland Fusiliers was raised by the Newcastle and Gateshead Chamber of Commerce and was known as the Newcastle Commercials.

The 17th Battalion was recruited from North Eastern Railway workers.

The regiment ended the war with five VCs but more than 16,000 men were killed.

In the Second World War five battalions of the Royal Northumberland Fusiliers were with the British Expeditionary Force.

The 1st Battalion was involved in the eight-month siege of Tobruk in North Africa and the 7th and 8th fought in Normandy.

The regiment later took part in the Korean War and actions against the Mau Mau in Kenya. In 1968 the Royal Northumberland Fusiliers was merged into the Royal Regiment of Fusiliers.

The museum bears testimony to this long history.

Among the exhibits is a Boer K96 Mauser carbine, a Dervish neck amulet, arrows and quiver, prayer board and clothing, a Prussian infantry officer's spiked helmet, a Chinese soldier's jacket from Korea and a Mau Mau rifle.

The museum is open from 11am-5pm daily until October 29 when it closes until April. Entry is free. Most users are also paying visitors to the castle, but people who want to specifically visit the museum can telephone (01665) 602152 in advance.

A bird's eye view of the priory can be had from a nearby 600ft hill which is crowned by another striking landmark.

This is the 80ft tall, highly ornate Brizlee Tower, Grade I listed and designed by Adam in 1781.

It was built by the First Duke as a memorial to his Duchess and also carries an inscription detailing his works in planting trees, especially beech and pine, and generally landscaping the park.

The tower has been recently restored.

The First Duchess laid out a series of carriage drives across the park, whose routes and names survive today.

Such excursions would need points of interest en route, such as the priory and a cave near the tower called Nine Year Old Hole, which was ornamented with carved figures.

"There was a nascent tourist industry in the 18th Century and you find places like the priory being mentioned by visitors writing about the North of England," says Mr Shrimpton.

In 1812 a triple-arched and decorative iron bridge was installed, followed by Park Farm in the 1820s by architect John Green, which became the Duke's home farm.

Exotic Indian cattle were also introduced to the park. According to Mr Shrimpton, the Indian connection began when the Third Duke married the great granddaughter of Clive of India.

As well as compounds of Indian cattle, different species of deer were also imported.

"You had quite a menagerie there," says Mr Shrimpton.

In 1859 the architect Anthony Salvin designed a forest lodge and entrance gateway on the Ratten Row approach from Alnwick.

Mr Shrimpton says: "Hulne Park is a remarkable place. Its beauty and the views are unbelievable.

"It is an experience anybody would always remember and I think it is one of the finest features of Northumberland.

"The public can enjoy good walks and have done so since it was opened up in the 19th Century.

"But it is probably less well known now in places like Tyneside than it was in the 19th Century, when there were fewer diversions and people set out on excursions to find out about places and enjoy a good day out in the fresh air."

Today farming, forestry and game shooting are the functions of the park. There is access by foot from 11am to sunset on most days of the year.

Cars, bikes and dogs are not allowed. A plan of the park is available from Alnwick tourist information office or by telephoning the estate office on (01665) 510771.

Brizlee Tower

The 7th Century crypt at Hexham Abbey

Hexham Abbey

Enter an underground chamber in the Northumberland market town of Hexham and, essentially, you step back to the 7th Century.

The steep stone stairway leads to chambers and passageways which make up the crypt of St Wilfrid's church, which he built on land given in about 672 by Queen Etheldreda, the wife of the Northumbrian king Ecgfrith.

This marked the beginning of the recorded history of the Northumberland market town.

Today, the crypt is beneath Hexham Abbey on a site which has been used for worship for 1,300 years. A descent into the crypt is to walk into a silent time capsule cut off from the whirl of the 21st Century above.

Wilfrid, Bishop of York, is likely to have brought back sacred relics from what would have been at that time an arduous journey to Rome. The place to house such relics would have been the crypt below the high altar of his church. From the central shrine and antechamber, passages radiate to north and south.

It is believed that one passage was used by monks and the other by pilgrims who had come to see the relics.

Illumination came from oil burning in scoops cut into the stone walls. A recess – still blackened – was hollowed out of the stone above the scoops so that the smoke would be contained and absorbed. This is early Christian Northumbria. But its history goes back even further.

The crypt walls were built using a ready-made quarry of dressed stones from the Roman settlement at nearby Corbridge.

Following recent

excavations and studies of the crypt stones, it is now thought that the material came from the ornamental stone bridge which crossed the Tyne and led to the Roman town of Coria at Corbridge.

One crypt stone shows the Roman olive leaf and berry pattern. Another slab records the dedication of a new granary by the Emperor Septimus Severus and his two sons, Caracalla and Geta, while they were in the North for their campaign into Scotland.

This stone has a story to tell. After the death of Severus at York, his sons inherited the Empire. But Caracalla had Geta killed and ordered that his name be removed from all inscriptions, which is what has happened on this stone.

Also used in the crypt is an altar to the god Maponus Apollo.

After the building of the 12th Century priory on the site, the crypt was lost to time.

But in 1725 it was rediscovered during the digging of foundations for a buttress to strengthen the abbey's tower. St Wilfrid's stone church – built with his knowledge of the architecture of Rome

There are fascinating features at every turn in Hexham Abbey, which reflect its long history.

None more so than the 9ft high sandstone slab which is one of the first sights to greet visitors.

Standing near the foot of the Night Stair, it is a dramatic tombstone to Flavinus, a standard bearer in a Roman cavalry troop in the 1st Century.

The inscription describes him as a horse soldier of the Cavalry Regiment of Petriana and standard bearer of the Troop of Candidus.

Flavinus died at the age of 25 after seven years' service.

He is shown wearing a plumed helmet, with cavalry sword and shield, and carrying a standard topped by a head surrounded by rays and which was probably an image of the Emperor.

His horse is rearing over a crouched, sword-clutching Briton.

The regiment was first raised in Gaul and served in Northumbria. It was decorated for gallantry and was granted the title "Emperor's Own".

The tombstone was found in 1881 beneath the floor of the entrance to the abbey.

Was Flavinus buried near the spot, and is the stone evidence of a Roman Hexham?

Or was the slab transported from Corbridge for use in the building of the church?

Whatever, the young cavalryman could not have imagined that almost 2,000 years in the future his name would be read by thousands of people annually.

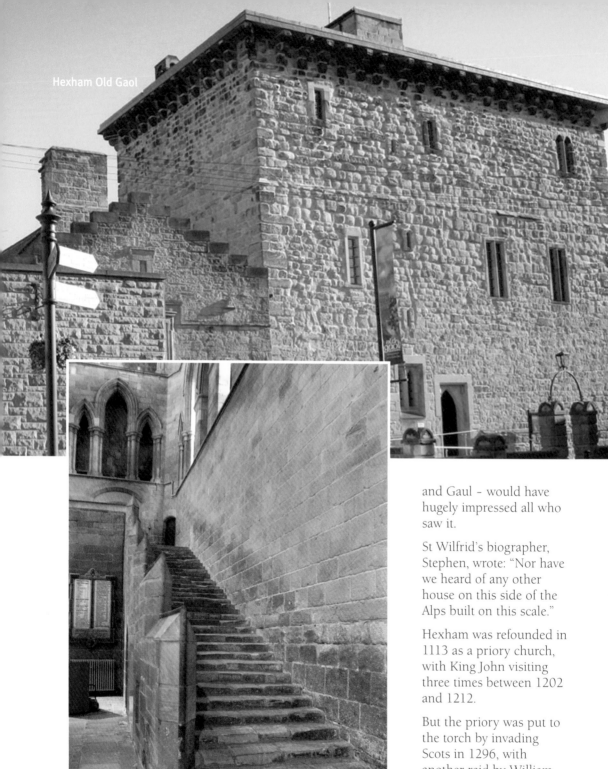

Hexham Old Gaol

The Night Stair

and Gaul – would have hugely impressed all who saw it.

St Wilfrid's biographer, Stephen, wrote: "Nor have we heard of any other house on this side of the Alps built on this scale."

Hexham was refounded in 1113 as a priory church, with King John visiting three times between 1202 and 1212.

But the priory was put to the torch by invading Scots in 1296, with another raid by William Wallace and his force the next year.

Turbulent times returned during the Wars of the

The dance of death paintings

Opposite the tombstone of Flavinus is what remains of an 8th Century carved cross, which is believed to have been a memorial to St Acca.

He accompanied St Wilfrid on his last journey to Rome and became Bishop of Hexham from 709-732.

It was recorded in the 12th Century that carved crosses were placed at the head and foot of Acca's grave.

A small cross shaft, which is also on show, was found at Spital, near Hexham, and has been described as that which marked the foot of the grave.

The large cross was rebuilt from three pieces found in different locations.

The central section was discovered in 1858 during demolition work on the abbey site, the top part in 1870 near St Mary's Church in the Market Place and the bottom slab in 1823 when it was being used as a door lintel in a farmhouse at Dilston.

In the middle of the Choir is the Frith Stool, or bishop's throne.

Probably dating from the 7th Century, it was carved from a single block of sandstone. Frith meant peace, and it may have also served as a symbol of sanctuary for fugitives.

On show in a niche is a tiny chalice, similar to those found in graves of 10th and 11th Century churchmen on the Continent.

The Hexham chalice was discovered in a coffin in 1860 when heating pipes were being installed in the abbey.

It was made of gilded copper alloy and was likely to have been used with a portable altar by travelling monks.

Behind the abbey lectern are four painted panels called the Dance of Death.

The 15th-Century paintings show Death, in the form of a skeleton, dancing with a cardinal, a king, an Emperor and the Pope.

Their purpose was to show how Death can visit individuals of any rank, at any time.

St Wilfrid appears to have been a colourful character of immense drive and energy.

Born into the Northumbria aristocracy, he entered the monastery on Lindisfarne at the age of 14 in 647.

After four years he left for Rome, staying at Lyons on the way.

During his years on the Continent, he built up his experiences of art and architecture, learning and song.

When he returned, St Wilfrid became a Church leader for 45 years, Bishop of York and of the Northumbrian people, founding the churches of Ripon and Hexham.

But St Wilfrid lived in uneasy times and his involvement in the lives of the Northumbrian royal family saw him deprived of his office, spending time imprisoned and travelling to Rome to appeal to the Pope for his reinstatement.

On the way this missionary bishop converted the pagans of Sussex and Frisia.

He also left a Christian legacy in the North of England and a church which is the heart of Hexham.

Hexham Abbey is open daily 9pm-5pm and has a gift shop. Visitors are asked to make a £3 voluntary donation. Tel: (01434) 602031.

After the abbey which dominates the centre of Hexham, one of the most arresting sights is the town's Old Gaol.

And if you are going to claim a national first then in Hexham's case it is that of having the earliest-recorded purpose-built prison in England.

It was constructed on the orders of William Melton, Archbishop of York, who ruled the roost in Hexham. It was complete by 1333 and the Archbishop thoughtfully provided manacles and fetters. John de Cawood cut loose from his career as a barber to take up the new job opportunity as gaoler at the wage of two pence a day.

For around 500 years the building, just off the Market Place, was used as a gaol, with prisoners taking the short walk for trial to the Moot Hall which was originally a fortified gateway guarding the Archbishop's Hall.

At the Old Gaol, the first and ground floors held prisoners who could afford to pay for better food and conditions. The dungeon, with its 20ft drop, held the poorest who relied on friends or the church for food.

The dungeon threw up a surprise during a recent £1.5m restoration project, which saw the Old Gaol re-open as a museum of Reiver, Border and Tynedale history.

When the concrete floor was taken up, Northumberland archaeologist Peter Ryder discovered a layer of mortared-together, heavy stone slabs. It is believed they were there to make the floor escape-proof. Peter says: "The effort of putting in a floor like this, presumably by candlelight, must have been immense and would have required motivation of the magnitude of enraged royalty."

Three escapes were recorded in the 16th Century, with the main break in 1538 after Henry VIII had taken over administration of the area. Royalty was enraged when, in the goal break, a Jesuit priest was among those freed by a band of horsemen. With religion a delicate issue at the time, the King ordered an investigation.

There was another breakout in 1559, and it is little wonder that the inmates were desperate to escape as disease and appalling conditions took their toll.

If they made it to the Moot Hall for sentence, the punishment meted out was often of a humiliating nature.

On show in the gaol are the stocks, where individuals were confined by the feet, and the pillory where they were held by the head. They had to accept what passers-by dealt them.

The use of the pillory was banned in 1837 and the stocks in the 1880s. The Market Place also had a whipping post but the practice was outlawed in 1817.

Perhaps the most notable exhibit is a skull believed to be that of Sir John Fenwick of Hexham, who was killed in 1644 in the English Civil War Battle of Marston Moor. Also on display is his helmet. Both helmet and skull have a hole in the same place.

The restoration was backed by a £968,000 Heritage Lottery Fund grant. The building is owned by Tynedale Council but is managed by the Historic Hexham Trust.

Roses when after a battle at nearby Devil's Water in 1464, the Lancastrians were defeated and the Duke of Somerset was beheaded in the Market Place and was buried in the church. Today's abbey has contributions from the 12th, 13th, 15th, 19th and 20th Centuries.

Inside, the finest view is from a gallery behind a stone parapet which is reached by the Night Stair.

For 800 years feet have trodden the 35 now-worn steps of the stair.

The Night Stair was used by the Augustinian priory canons who were woken in the early hours and descended from their dormitory to say prayers and sing psalms in the choir.

The Night Stair is a rare survivor, and it is still used today for services.

Traces of lead can still be seen on the steps, believed to be from the 1296 raid when fire melted the lead on the roof.

The 7th Century Bishop's Throne

The Rector of Hexham, the Rev Graham Usher, says: "It is a building which has a sense of the prayers of generations soaked into its walls. There is heritage and history and a sense of our forebears, but the building is not a museum piece. It is a living church and the historic parts of the abbey are still used today. The building had a profound impact, with the town growing up around it."

The abbey attracts 120,000 visitors a year. Tourism revenue is important. It costs £250,000 a year to run and maintain the building and all funds are raised locally and through visitors.

Mr Usher says: "We are incredibly privileged to have such a building which is such a mix of styles and history. We are still living out the story today."

While the history of Hexham Abbey spans 1,300 years, one of its newest exhibits brings the story of the town up to date.

The Millennium banner is the work of about 40 members of Hexham Embroiderers' Guild.

At the centre is the name Hexham in Celtic-style lettering. It overlies depictions of the wide Northumbrian skies, hills and moors, woodlands, the town's skyscape with the abbey prominent, groups of young and older people and the River Tyne.

There are 46 smaller panels showing the factory, wildlife, Hexham's Moot Hall, a market stall in The Shambles, the Temperley Fountain, a Hexham doorway, park bandstand, the abbey chalice and rosette stone, Hexham races, cattle at the mart, St Andrew's Cross, and Roman soldiers on Hadrian's Wall.

Its rich colours and the craft of its diverse images prove that the same creativity which produced the historic carvings and paintings which adorn the abbey is as vibrant today as it ever was.

Tynemouth Castle and Priory

For both monks and the military, the prominent headland at the mouth of the Tyne was the place to be.

From Penbal Crag, ships approaching the river could be seen from a great distance, while on a clear day the view up and down the coast can extend to the Farne Islands off Northumberland.

Excavations in the 1960s revealed traces of at least one large Iron Age roundhouse.

Such special coastal areas were favoured as monastery and church sites, as at Lindisfarne, Hartlepool and Whitby, and the crag at Tynemouth was no different.

It was the site of a 7th Century monastery and later of Tynemouth Priory.

But the headland was of strategic importance to the military and the priory site also became a castle.

Religious and military communities lived cheek by jowl until the Dissolution of the monasteries in 1539.

"The curtain wall of the castle was the cloister wall of the priory and the gatehouse keep was also the gatehouse to the priory," says English Heritage's Tynemouth site manager Stephen Laidler, one of whose previous jobs has been that of hill shepherd.

"You have soldiers living on the same spot as monks and I can't believe that they got on very well together."

In fact, for many years the headland bristled with guns.

It is separated from the river mouth by a lower ledge of land called the Spanish Battery.

In between is Prior's Haven, a protected landing place for whoever occupied the headland.

When the priory was

dissolved, the site became part of Henry VIII's national defence network and plans were laid to turn it into a fortress to command the entrance to the Tyne.

Mercenaries from the Spanish army were employed in 1545 to man guns on the lower promontory – hence the name.

The later armament on the Spanish Battery, two six-inch guns and two quick-firing six-pounders, were not dismantled until the 1950s, along with those from the headland.

During the Napoleonic Wars there were 51 guns at Tynemouth and in 1881 there were still 20.

The site remained manned and fully operational during the two world wars.

By 1914, a 9.2in gun which took 15 men to operate had been sited on the headland with a range of 12,000 yards to fire on warships.

Next to the 9.2 position are the concrete emplacements for two six-inch guns, each manned by a 13-strong team.

In 1993, a six-inch gun which had been made at Vickers Armstrong's Newcastle works, and similar to those deployed on the headland during the Second World War,

The Christian history of the headland dates from the late 7th Century monastery, which was plundered by the Vikings in AD800 and eventually destroyed in AD 875.

Robert de Mowbray, Earl of Northumberland, refounded the monastery in 1085 as a Benedictine Priory dependant on St Alban's Abbey in Hertfordshire.

The building of the priory is thought to have begun by 1090.

The Norman church was enlarged between 1195-1220. The ruins of the presbytery still stand to the height of 73ft.

Projecting from the east end of the church is a small, vaulted 15th Century chapel called St Mary's Chapel or the Percy Chantry.

It was restored by architect John Dobson with William Wailes, of Saltwell Towers in Gateshead, providing the stained glass windows and is the most complete part of the church.

Of the monastic buildings, the Prior's Chapel survives and contains a collection of carved stones from the priory buildings.

Tynemouth was one of the wealthier religious sites and accommodated Edward II, Edward III and Richard II.

The site had another function in addition to the monastic and military and that was as a navigational role for shipping.

There is a 16th Century record of a light in the form of a coal fire in an open brazier at the top of a turret of the church. It may also be the case that, due to its value as a navigational aid, the east end of the church was retained to its full height after the Dissolution.

A lighthouse tower was erected in 1664 and rebuilt in 1775, with an oil lamp and rotating reflectors installed in 1802.

The lighthouse was demolished in 1898 and was replaced by those at St Mary's Island off Whitley Bay and Souter at Whitburn.

St Mary's Chapel

was installed on the emplacement.

Underneath are the ammunition magazines, complete with shell hoists, which are open to the public on summer weekends.

There were still more guns, including two 12-pounder quick firers and a four-inch "interrogation" gun to warn shipping.

Overlooking King Edward's Bay on the north side of the headland is an 1859 six-inch muzzle-loading cannon which was the subject of trials by the army to see if its smooth barrel could be rifled to increase its range and accuracy.

It was installed to celebrate the centenary of the Tynemouth Volunteer Artillery.

Finally, on the southern flank of the headland were two 12-pound 1904 rapid fire guns.

Tynemouth was the

A letter from a monk, almost certainly from Tynemouth's mother house at St Albans, gives a colourful impression of life on the headland in the 13th Century.

"Our house is confined to the top of a high rock and is surrounded by the sea on every side but one.

"Day and night the waves break and roar. Thick sea frets roll in wrapping everything in gloom. Dim eyes, hoarse voices, sore throats are the consequence.

"Spring and summer never come here. The north wind is always blowing and brings with it cold and snow; or storms in which the wind tosses the salt sea in masses over our buildings.

"In the spring the sea air blights the blossoms of the stunted fruit trees, so that you think yourself lucky to find a wizened apple, though it will set your teeth on edge should you try to eat it.

"See to it, dear brother, that you do not come to this comfortless place. But the church is of wondrous beauty. It has lately been completed.

"We are well off for food, thanks to the abundant supply of fish of which we tire."

controlling hub of coastal defences from Blyth to batteries south of Sunderland.

The gun emplacements and magazines at Tynemouth are now among the last examples of British coastal fortification and among the best preserved of the period.

They were the latest manifestation of the headland's long defensive role.

The site was fortified by the late 11th Century when Robert de Mowbray held out at Tynemouth for two months after his rebellion against the King, William Rufus.

In 1296 Tynemouth was given formal permission by the Crown to fortify and the work involved one of the largest areas of fortification in England in the shape of 3,200ft of wall.

The Tynemouth headland is reputed to have been the burial place of three kings.

It is thought that St Oswin, the 7th Century murdered king of Deira which later became part of the kingdom of Northumbria, was buried at Tynemouth.

A shrine to St Oswin, to whom miracles were attributed, became a place of pilgrimage.

St Osred, another murdered king of Northumbria, was buried at Tynemouth, as was King Malcolm III of Scotland after his defeat and death at Alnwick in 1093.

His body is believed to have been moved later to Dunfermline Abbey.

The headland was used as the parish burial ground and there are almost 700 gravestones, mainly dating from 1715 to 1856.

Among them is that of Alexander Rollo, who held the lantern at the burial of Sir John Moore who was killed at the Battle of Corunna in the Napoleonic Peninsula war.

Alexander, a corporal in the Royal Regiment of Artillery, risked enemy fire by holding the lantern and the event was the subject of a painting and the poem by Charles Wolfe. Sir John was the commander of the British forces in Portugal and advanced into Spain after the French took Madrid.

It is believed that Alexander was based at Tynemouth castle and married a local girl. They had 11 children.

He served in the army for 26 years, returned to Tynemouth and was sextant of the local church and showed visitors around the priory ruins. He died in 1856 aged 82.

The present gatehouse was built in the 1390s and in 1544 Tynemouth was the base for the English fleet involved in the invasion of Scotland.

In 1640 the castle was taken and garrisoned by the Scots and in later years was used for French and Dutch prisoners of war.

Early photographs show how military buildings cluttered the interior. Guns and munitions were stacked against the priory ruins and a huge powder magazine was built on the site of the cloister.

When the military moved out in 1960, the interior of the castle was opened out and grassed and English Heritage took over in 1984.

Tynemouth Priory and Castle is open from April 1-September 30 daily from 10am-6pm, October 1-31 daily from 10am-4pm, and November 1-March 31 Thursday-Monday from 10am-4pm.

Telephone (0191) 257-1090.

Lady's Well

Even in a county as lushly green as Northumberland, one spot stands out - where the overwhelming sensation is one of coming across an oasis.

It is at the end of a short stroll from the village of Holystone in Upper Coquetdale in Northumberland National Park.

Standing amid the fields and farmland is a copse of trees which shade Lady's Well, cared for by the National Trust.

The well is fed by a natural spring, producing crystal-clear water at the rate of 530 gallons a minute. It never freezes or runs dry.

Such a site was probably held to be a sacred place in prehistoric times and these were often adopted by Christianity.

The walk to the well follows a stream which, at the right time of year, is flanked by sheets of yellow mimulus blooms.

The spring water is contained in a substantial stone tank, with a 19th Century stone cross and a 15th Century statue - brought from Alnwick in 1788 - of St Paulinus, who is said to have baptised converts at the site.

The name Lady's Well came from a small Benedictine nunnery founded in 1124 at Holystone, and which was taken over by the Augustinians in the 13th Century. An old belief is that an altar-shaped stone near the well is the 'holy' stone which gave the village its name.

The stone appears in an account of a visit to the well in 1715 by the antiquary John Warburton, who says: "Out of the well floweth a ...stream of water very cold, and clear as christall, and would be a most commodious cold

The approach to Lady's Well

Upper Coquetdale is rich in the archaeology left behind by the generations who lived in this beautiful part of Northumberland for thousands of years.

That history has been explored in the Upper Coquetdale Community Archaeology Project, run by Northumberland National Park, with the National Trust, Northumberland County Council and Rothbury Local History Society.

Locals joined archaeologists to investigate a 50ft long mound above Harehaugh Iron Age hillfort, which dates from 2,300 years ago.

The heavily-defended hillfort dominates the confluence of the Grasslees Burn and the River Coquet – a strategic point for movement between Redesdale and Coquetdale.

Fifty people took part in the dig, which revealed the mound is a long burial cairn from the earlier Neolithic period.

The Neolithic people, no doubt impressed by the panoramic views, had added material to the existing rock ridge to create a lengthy, pyramid-shaped structure in which burials were made.

Another excavation looked at the site of a deserted medieval village on National Trust land at Low Trewhitt.

On a south-facing slope above Thropton, Low Trewhitt farm sits at the confluence of two burns which flow into the River Coquet. But the farm, part of the National Trust's Cragside estate, is in a landscape full of platforms, bumps and troughs below the grass.

This was a setting that had provided a good living for thousands of years, as suggested by a nearby prehistoric burial mound, excavated at the turn of the last century.

Historical records indicate that a village existed here in the medieval period. Next to the site, is a field with the visible remains of medieval ploughing. Ridges and furrows show as bold corrugations in the pasture.

Under the direction of Durham University's Archaeological Services, local volunteers investigated the site to see if there was a village at all and, if so, how old it was and why it was abandoned.

Large stone-based platforms and cobbled streets laid out in a grid pattern were revealed, along with over 100 pottery finds dating to the 12th and 18th Centuries.

This indicates that the site was probably laid out in the 1100s and at some stage, most likely the 15th Century, it fell into disuse, only to be re-occupied again as a farm in the 18th Century.

Low Trewhitt is one of scores of deserted medieval villages in Northumberland.

County archaeologist Chris Burgess says: "A lot of farms and smaller villages are what remains of much bigger settlements.

"We know a lot of deserted villages existed from documentary evidence. The house platforms at Low Trewhitt, the grid of roads which had drainage and metalled surfaces, means it must have been quite a community."

According to Chris, a number of factors could have contributed to villages going out of existence.

These may include conflict, disease and changes in land ownership and management.

As agriculture became more sophisticated and smaller tenancies were absorbed into bigger farms, there was less need for manpower.

Chris says: "At places like Low Trewhitt, you stand and think about what must have been quite a bustling community, and now it's gone."

St Mungo's Well, Holystone

Woodhouses Bastle

bath and perhaps effect several cures.

"At the east end lyeth a stone called the holy stone, said to be the same whereon the Bishop (Paulinus) kneeled at his baptising of the heathen English, and was formerly held in great veneration by the gentry of the Roman Catholick religion who ofttimes come here on pilgrimage."

What is left of the nunnery survives at St Mary's Church in the village on a site where worship has taken place for 1,400 years. The church was rebuilt in the mid-19th Century. In

its grounds, a grave is encased by metal bars to protect it from body snatchers.

Three grave slabs are evidence of medieval life in Holystone.

The nunnery had 27 occupants in 1313, but it would have been a vulnerable place in the centuries of border conflict. By the time of the Dissolution in 1536, there were only eight nuns and the house was worth just over £11.

Near the church is St Mungo's Well. The Celtic saint is said to have

travelled through Holystone on his journey from Wales to Scotland.

Lady's Well was also known as St Ninian's Well, after the 5th Century apostle and Bishop of Whithorn in Scotland.

The story is that Paulinus baptised 3,000 converts at the site on Easter Day in 627, although there is no archaeological evidence to support this claim.

What is more certain is that, in 627, Paulinus baptised the Northumbrian King Edwin in York.

The Venerable Bede

Statue of St Paulinus at Lady's Well

records that Paulinus visited what is now Northumberland and baptised people in the River Glen at the Ad Gefrin palace site at the base of Yeavering Bell in the Cheviot Hills.

Whatever, the long holy associations surrounding the village and the well give the site a deeply contemplative and peaceful atmosphere.

The well was, into the last century, still used for the superstitious and perhaps pagan-origin custom of dropping crooked pins into the water and making a wish.

The practice was also carried out at the pin well near Wooler, where a restoration project recently took place.

Old habits die hard, as the coins in any wishing well today illustrate.

Lady's Well, a scheduled ancient monument, also had a practical use. It is sited near the Roman road running from Bremenium fort in Redesdale, and is likely to have been a watering place.

Back in the village is the 17th Century former Salmon Inn, now a private home.

At the opposite end of the village from the well is the Forestry Commission's Holystone Wood car park, which is the starting point for walks.

If Holystone has echoes of holiness and calm, then the nearby Woodhouses Bastle represents the other side of the coin, which was the need for protection in violent times. The bastle has been restored by the National Park Authority and there is a public access footpath.

A stone above the door is dated 1602 and carries the letters WP BP TAM, which is probably a reference to William Potte or Potts, who owned land locally.

This was a top-of-the-range bastle which had the

luxury of internal stairs and a slop stone, or forerunner of the kitchen sink.

Also falling into the category of superior residence is nearby Holystone Grange, an impressive turreted building which began life as a farmhouse.

In 1897 it was bought by Newcastle architect Frank Rich, who extended it and turned it into a Tudor-style mansion.

The garden was fashioned in the 1930s, using stone balustrades and material from Haggerston Castle near Berwick which was being demolished.

Like Woodhouses Bastle, Holystone Grange must have one of the best views of any house in Britain – over the River Coquet and the surrounding hills.

Holystone is reached by the B6341 off the A68 via Elsdon or by the B6341 from Thropton via Hepple. Low Cleughs is off the Bellingham-West Woodburn road off the A68.

Harbottle Castle

History has been harsher on some Northumbrian castles than others.

Today, what is left of Harbottle Castle stands as a picturesque ruin on a long spur of land above the River Coquet.

"It was once a very big castle," says James Crow, senior lecturer at Newcastle University who led digs on the site, commissioned by Northumberland National Park, over two years from 1997.

In the 14th Century, a barbican, or outer defensive structure guarding the entrance to a castle, was built along with a drawbridge and was likely to have been modelled on Alnwick Castle.

It probably demonstrates the rivalry between the two castles as the power bases for the Umfravilles at Harbottle and the Percys at Alnwick.

Harbottle was a sufficiently important fortress in 1515 to be chosen to accommodate Margaret Tudor, who was the widow of James IV of Scotland and the sister of Henry VIII.

She arrived at Harbottle to give birth to her daughter, also Margaret, who grew up to be grandmother of James VI of Scotland and James I of England and Scotland.

It is said that Margaret Tudor brought 22 gowns of gold and silk with her, and sent to Edinburgh for more.

Harbottle was strategically placed to control movement through Coquetdale to and from Scotland, and into Redesdale.

Such a raised platform over a river could well have

Matt Offer

A prominent feature of the skyline crags overlooking Harbottle village is the Drake Stone.

This is a huge Fell Sandstone boulder of more than 2,000 tonnes and 30ft in height.

Inscriptions carved on the boulder, dating from the 19th Century, show that people have long been drawn to the stone.

Local folklore maintained that the Drake Stone has the power to heal ailing children and that youngsters passed over the rock would be cured.

An 1873 handbook of Durham and Northumberland describes the Drake Stone as "a very interesting relic, being the Draag Stone of the Druids. The custom still prevailing in Harbottle of passing sick children over the Drake Stone may be a relic of Druidical times".

On open moorland behind the stone is the lonely tarn of Harbottle Lough. Local belief that the Drake Stone was invested with powers may be linked to the nearby lough and the conviction of prehistoric people that water bodies were the entrances to another world.

The Drake Stone can be reached by walking from the Forestry Commission car park on the edge of the village through Northumberland Wildlife Trust's Harbottle Crags nature reserve.

Those who make the ascent are rewarded with memorial seats at different levels from which to enjoy the sweeping views over and beyond the Coquet Valley.

Nearby is a quarry where millstones were fashioned from the 16th to the 19th Centuries.

The remains of millstones which never made it can be found along with sledge tracks caused by the transportation of the stones.

been a fortified site before the building of the castle.

Indeed, the name Harbottle may be derived from here-botl, meaning army building.

After the Norman invasion, land in Northumberland was granted to the Umfravilles, who had castles at Prudhoe and Elsdon.

By 1157 it was recorded that the Umfravilles were at Harbottle. The territory was granted so that it could be defended from "enemies and wolves".

In 1174 Harbottle failed its first test when it was taken by the Scottish King William the Lion after he had failed at Carlisle and Prudhoe castles.

He quickly lost Harbottle when he was captured at Alnwick. Harbottle performed better in 1296, when it resisted another siege, but in 1318 it was captured by Robert the Bruce.

No doubt not wishing to have to repeat the feat, he ordered demolition work on the castle.

The 1990s digs produced good evidence that the whole of the outer wall of the castle had been knocked down and toppled into the castle ditch, making Harbottle half the fortress it had been.

Harbottle Lough

Harbottle became a healthier place when the peace which followed centuries of conflict settled on the village and made the castle redundant.

David Dippie Dixon, in his 1903 book Upper Coquetdale, tells of Dr Richardson, the 19th Century medical man for Harbottle and district.

Dr Richardson wrote to The Times on the health and longevity of the Upper Coquet population.

In 1874, he recorded that of 106 deaths in the parish, more than a quarter were of individuals over 80 years old.

In days when child mortality was commonplace, he says: "In the village of Harbottle there were 37 children and during the last 20 years no child has died.

"I may add another instance of the large proportion of children existing and their immunity from death. A farmer in this parish and his three shepherds who have occupied their present situations nearly 30 years have among them 47 children and not a single death has occurred in these families.

"The inhabitants have abundance of plain, substantial food, excellent water, good residences as a rule and regular but not severe work in a pure bracing atmosphere and are highly intelligent and generally abstemious."

Ironically, for one so concerned with the statistics of mortality, Dr Richardson called his greyhound Dr Death. He erected a monument to the dog in the garden of his home.

But Harbottle was the subject of major rebuilding in the 14th and 15th Centuries as a key defence against the Scots and Reivers.

The castle passed to the Tailbois family. But William Tailbois chose the wrong side in the Wars of the Roses and was executed after the Battle of Hexham in 1464, and the castle was forfeit.

The vulnerability of castles to gunpowder and artillery had been demonstrated by the Scottish King James IV, who had successfully

The central role of the castle in the history of Harbottle was celebrated in a project by Northumberland National Park, which manages the Grade I listed site.

The project involved children from Harbottle School, who wrote poems about the castle.

The work of two of the youngsters was carved on a sandstone block and a stone seat created by Hexham master stonemason David Edwick and sited near the castle entrance.

The poem on the block, The Sad Castle, by eight-year-old Felicity Lance, asked the question "Who made me into a ruin?"

Felicity's work was chosen by the then Poet Laureate Ted Hughes to win the national W H Smith Young Writers competition, which drew 30,000 entries.

Fellow eight-year-old pupil Robert Corley's poem, Old Castle, was carved on to the stone seat.

THE SAD CASTLE

WHO MADE ME
INTO A RUIN
LIKE AN OLD CITY?

WAS IT THE SOLDIERS
WHO RODE OUT
ON HORSEBACK?

WAS IT MY OLD ENEMY
THE SCOTS?

OR WAS IT THOSE
BORDER REIVERS?

PERHAPS IT WAS
JUST THE CENTURIES
PASSING

FELICITY
LANCE
HARBOTTLE C.E. FIRST SCHOOL
MCMXCVIII

employed the weapons against the castles at Wark, Ford, Etal and Chillingham before being killed in the rout of the Battle of Flodden in 1513.

Around 25 years later Henry VIII began building artillery fortifications and Harbottle was supplied with gun ports, some of which survive today.

"It is one of the major examples of re-fortification using artillery," says James Crow.

After the Union of the Crowns in 1603, the castle became redundant and in 1635 it was acquired by the Widdrington family.

Edward Widdrington built a house in the village, which he called Harbottle Castle, and mostly used stone from the original.

Circumstances had come full circle since the 1990s excavations showed that some of the stone for the rebuilding of the castle had come from the nunnery at nearby Holystone.

"There had to be the will to maintain the castle and to do that would have taken a huge investment," says James.

"If nobody was willing to do that at Harbottle, the castle's days were numbered."

Shillmoor and Upper Coquetdale

There are views you can take in on the hoof, others where you are persuaded to pause and take a mental snapshot.

But in the high country of Upper Coquetdale in Northumberland, there is one vista which virtually forces the observer to sit down for half an hour and simply drink it all in.

Aim for Alwinton, the last village on the journey to the head of the River Coquet - Northumberland's longest waterway which winds for 55 miles to the sea at Amble.

For a settlement which was for so long in the front line of the Scots-English tug of war, the local inn is diplomatically called the Rose and Thistle after the emblems of the two countries.

A mile beyond the inn is a right of way signpost to Shillmoor which directs walkers up Pass Peth.

This path edges up the side of the hill and reaches a ridge, where a stunning panorama unfolds, revealing the young River Coquet winding its way down the valley, with hills rolling in from right and left.

Solitary in this broad, captivating canvas is Shillmoor Farm.

Down below, to the left of a ford, is the site of the deserted medieval village of Linbriggs.

The outline of the imprints of around 15 buildings can be discerned, and boundary lines. Old accounts speak of a mill.

It is a stencil, a blueprint, of what was once a community living its life beside the river.

But, like Alwinton, the village was vulnerable to raiders, and this may be the reason for abandonment.

There is a 16th Century record of complaints lodged with officialdom by Alwinton and Linbriggs, protesting that the Armstrongs, Elliots, and Crosiers were among around 200 raiders who stole 100 cattle, 20 horses and took 20 local men prisoner.

Descending from the ridge, the path follows the river, passing circular drystone

stells, where sheep can be gathered.

Shillmoor is a good example of the sort of sturdy, substantial farmhouses which were built in Northumberland in the late 18th and early 19th Centuries.

With raiding now firmly in the past, land was enclosed as part of the widespread development of agriculture.

In fact, Shillmoor represents the first permanent settlement in this part of Upper Coquetdale since medieval days.

To fully appreciate the wide skies and liberating sense of space, strike up the hill just before the farm to Copper Snout, towards Kidland Forest.

To the left is the Otterburn Range and ahead the Cheviots Hills.

Astonishingly, this landscape with the touch of the wild is only 45 miles from Tyneside. But it is a world away.

The return leg to Alwinton is by Clennell Street, recorded in medieval times as a major route across the Cheviots and an old salt and drove road.

The Salt Tax, which was not repealed until 1825, meant smuggling was rife.

There is a belief that

The wild expanses of Upper Coquetdale demand respect, especially in bad weather conditions.

On the high land at Shiel Bog, above the village of Alnham, is a 30-inch high memorial stone which reads: "Eleanor Heron, departed December 3rd 1863."

Hairdresser Paul Renton, who is related to the Heron clan, made a pilgrimage to the remote spot after details emerged during family tree research.

Paul learned that his great great grandmother Eleanor had died at the age of 50 after being caught in a severe snowstorm as she crossed the hills from Alnham to Hartside.

"She must have gone into the dip in the ground for shelter," says Paul.

"It was quite an emotional moment to find the stone. It is in good condition bearing in mind that it has been there for almost 150 years and it is such a wild place.

"I wanted to make sure it was not forgotten and that it stays as a little piece of history."

Eleanor is referred to in records as an apothecary and wife of John Heron, tenant at Hartside Farm.

She is described as being "well known and respected".

Rory is a name which has become part and parcel of the folklore of Upper Coquetdale.

Rory's Still is the best known of several illegal whisky operations in the remoteness of these high lands.

Stiff duties had been imposed by the Tippling Act of 1751 and that made illicit whisky production and smuggling an attractive proposition.

In England in 1803, the duty on a gallon of whisky was eight shillings and three shillings in Scotland.

In the 1830s, 53 officers were employed in the Borders in a bid to prevent whisky smuggling.

In 1822, it was reported that an illicit still discovered in the hills at Tosson overlooking the River Coquet, was capable of turning out 100 gallons of spirit a week.

It is believed that illegal distillation continued in Upper Coquetdale until at least 1870.

The late Newcastle local historian John Philipson carried out a study of illicit whisky ventures in Upper Coquetdale.

Six illegal distillery sites had been recorded a century ago - Rory's Still at Inner Hare Cleugh, Rowhope, Carlcroft, Saugh Rig, Kitty's Walls and Blindburn.

John Philipson tackled the sites at Inner Hare Cleugh, Saugh Rig and Blindburn.

Rory's Still consisted of a kiln built against the slope of the hill and the remains of a building where the distillation took place.

A turf roof would probably have continued the steep incline of the hillside for concealment purposes.

The site at Blindburn consisted of a rectangular building with a kiln at one end.

Saugh Rig is just above Shillmoor on the Wholehope Burn, with coal and barley for the production process

arriving by pack pony from Clennell Street and the spirits leaving the same way.

The site is hidden in a deep cleft in the burn, 1,100 ft above sea level.

A phial used for sampling the spirit, which would have been attached to a piece of string and lowered into the bung hole of the keg, was unearthed.

There was a ready local market. It is recorded how Northumberland Archdeacon Sharp criticised the drinking habits of the farmers and shepherds of Upper Coquetdale.

The historian MacKenzie commented on heavy whisky drinking in the area, stating that the locals were "fond of strong liquors, which exhilarate the spirits, and by a temporary madness, vary the uniform circulation of thought."

Which is one way to describe getting completely bladdered.

Clennell Street was a main track well before the medieval period.

This is strengthened by the remains of a number of prehistoric settlements near the route including, not far from Alwinton, the hill fort of Camp Knowe.

The impression that this is a land set apart is reinforced by local place names such as Kyloe Shin, Inner Quickening Cleugh, Murder Cleugh,

Bloodybush Edge, Flesh Shank, Sneer Hill, Cushat Law, Gowkhope Shank, The Slime and Beefstand, where it is believed Reivers hid cattle before driving them over the border.

Further up the valley past Shillmoor, there is another wild walk to Windy Gyle, following an old drove road called The Street.

The starting point for this walk is the site of the former 18th Century,

charmingly-named Slyme Foot pub, a drovers' haunt.

Near Windy Gyle is Russell's Cairn, named after Lord Francis Russell, who is said to have been killed at the site when a meeting between Scots and English to discuss grievances ended in affray.

Today, Windy Gyle is visited for its sweeping views and soothing silence.

Hardwick Park in its 18th Century heyday

Hardwick Park

In the 18th Century, Hardwick Park in County Durham was the height of fashion.

It was developed as extensive pleasure gardens with a lake, serpentine river, and a series of classical and Gothic buildings.

Stowe in Buckinghamshire, Stourhead in Wiltshire, Studley Royal in North Yorkshire and Gibside in Tyne and Wear are examples of the enthusiasm for water features, temples, towers and grottoes.

For many years, Hardwick slipped into decay and obscurity but, remarkably, its skeleton survived and the park is now triumphantly making a comeback in an £8m restoration scheme by Durham County Council.

The Friends of Hardwick were formed in 1998 to help in the resurrection and Tony Blair agreed to serve as their president as the park is in his Sedgefield constituency.

The re-emergence of Hardwick has been recognised by English Heritage with a grade two-star listing as an historic landscape.

And Hardwick can claim to be the only known example of a park where all the ornamental buildings were designed by James Paine, the leading architect of the day.

Paine's Hardwick included a Banqueting House, Gothic seat, bath house, a woodland hideaway known as the Bono Retiro, a temple, Gothic bridge, mock Gothic castle and a grotto.

The lake, serpentine, ponds, Grand Terrace and a circular walk completed the picture.

Hardwick was paid for by John Burdon, who created the park between 1748 and 1792.

He was undoubtedly a lucky man. After all, he was the youngest boy in a family of 18 children and still managed to inherit his merchant father's estate of £140,000 in 1748 as the only surviving son.

In the same year, he bought land at Hardwick for £10,800 from Lord Lambton, who had six daughters to marry off.

Burdon took over Hardwick Hall, which is now a hotel. He set about fashioning a landscape which would mightily impress his visitors and – against the grain of the times – also allowed in the locals for guided tours.

He also bought nearby Coxhoe Hall, where the poet Elizabeth Barrett Browning was born in 1806. Tony Smith, Durham County Council countryside group manager, says: "Places like Hardwick showed how wealthy you were. Features from the surrounding countryside were 'borrowed', as was the case at Hardwick where views

A Hardwick mystery which is unlikely to ever be solved turns on the disappearance of the statue of Neptune which stood on an island in the serpentine until the early 1950s.

The statue was made of lead on an iron frame and rumours abound as to its fate.

One was that it was dragged off its island when the Army left and ended up in an officer's garden in the south of England.

Another was that it had sunk into the silt of the bed of the serpentine as it was being floated off the island on a raft. Divers tested this theory but found nothing.

The Gothic Seat at Hardwick Park

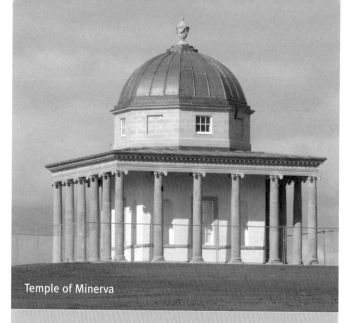
Temple of Minerva

The Circuit Walk at Hardwick was designed to create a deliberate sequence of happenings, with the 15-acre lake the biggest feature.

Archaeological work on the old lake dam revealed a lime slaking pit which had been used to produce mortar for the park's buildings, and a system for providing a cascade.

A fine view of the lake would be had from the Grand Terrace – 21ft wide and a third of a mile long. Off the Grand Terrace is the roofed and arched Gothic seat, which fronts on to the Round Pool.

At the end of the terrace was the bath house, with Doric columns. It had changing rooms for both sexes at the sides of an oval bath finished in blue mosaic tiles and fed by lake water – probably heated by a wood-burning boiler. It is hoped the bath house will be rebuilt if funding can be raised.

Next port of call was Bona Retiro, or place of pleasant retirement, which was hidden in woodland and in front of which was the Bottle Pond.

The first floor library was lit by stained glass windows and there were busts of Isaac Newton, Francis Bacon, John Locke, Marcus Aurelius, Robert Boyle and Marcus Cicero.

The Bottle Pond lay below the lake cascade, which was reflected in a mirror at the entrance to Bona Retiro.

The park's showpiece, the Temple of Minerva sited on its hill, is thought to be based on the mausoleum of Diocletian in Split on the Dalmatian coast. In the temple stood Minerva, goddess of wisdom and war, and its 18ft cubic room with lead dome housed busts of Homer, Virgil, Horace, Milton, Shakespeare, Dryden, Ben Johnson and Alexander the Great.

Crossing the rebuilt Gothic bridge over the serpentine, the view is of the 50ft Gothic castle. Along the serpentine are remains of the Gothic grotto which would also be rebuilt, as would a Banqueting House, if a £4m second phase is possible.

were created of the tower of Sedgefield church.

"John Burdon developed Hardwick in the grand 18th Century manner" says Tony.

In 1790, he sold Hardwick to MP William Russell of Brancepeth Castle and, in 1828, it passed to the Seventh Lord Boyne, remaining in the family until the 1920s. But by the 1860s, the lake had silted up and disappeared, and the buildings deteriorated.

The Banqueting House was demolished in 1947 and the stonework was used to build the facade of a cinema in nearby Trimdon Village.

When the cinema in its turn was knocked down, the material was reclaimed and is in storage in the hope that the Banqueting Hall can be rebuilt.

Hardwick Hall became a Bevan Boys' hostel in the Second World War, an Army training base, and then a maternity home.

The parkland was divided in the 1960s by the A177 bypass. In 1972, it appeared that Hardwick's fortunes were changing when Durham County Council bought 50 acres in the south-west corner of the park. But the council later considered that the buildings were a danger to the public and planned their demolition.

View across lake to Hardwick Hall

It sparked a local outcry, with Sedgefield Civic Society leading the fight to save the structures.

The council's plans were thrown out after a public inquiry in 1981.

"I don't think the value of what was left was understood at the time," says Tony Smith.

The first step on the road to recovery was the rebuilding of the Gothic bridge, which won an award.

Then, in 1996, Sedgefield doctor Peter Jones, while out walking, came across the remains of the bath house in ground which had been disturbed.

The Heritage Lottery Fund contributed almost £5m and the council also chipped in. Another 150 acres, embracing all of the historic park, were bought. Included was East Park on the other side of the A177.

Hardwick, with its walks, serpentine and population of ducks, swans and coots, attracts 250,000 visitors a year.

The Chantry at Morpeth

Morpeth Castles, Chantry and Clock

Sounds can be just as much a part of the spirit of a place as the sights.

Out on the hills and moors of the North-East, the bubbling sound of the curlew or the skylark's uplifting melody enrich the experience.

Another sound which encapsulates the often haunting beauty of the region is man-made – that of the Northumbrian small pipes.

And Morpeth in Northumberland is privileged to have an internationally-important collection of Northumbrian pipes which are of as much interest to students of the archaeology of music in Britain as they are to the general visitor.

The collection of bagpipes, which also includes Scots, Irish and other instruments from across Europe, is held in Morpeth's medieval Chantry building. Dating from the late 13th Century, the Chantry has had a chequered existence and, as well as the bagpipes, it houses the town's visitor information and Northumbrian crafts centres.

The core of the bagpipes collection was built up by William Alfred Cocks and numbers around 120

Morpeth Court House

instruments, to which the Chantry has added another 30 with the earliest dating from the 17th Century.

It is both an archive and a tribute to the clear, sweet sound of the Northumbrian pipes, which occupy a key place in the region's cultural heritage and identity.

"People are usually amazed at how bagpipes are found across Europe. They have been about for a long time - Shakespeare mentions them and Chaucer's miller played them," says collection curator Anne Moore. "But in England it is only the Northumbrian pipes which have survived. You don't get Yorkshire pipes or Surrey pipes. It is something to be proud of."

The Chantry in Morpeth began life as a bridge chapel and is one of only a handful to have survived.

Crossing water and travelling has long been an activity requiring good luck and blessings.

The Romans would habitually throw offerings from bridges into rivers to earn good fortune on journeys.

The priest in the bridge chapel would also bless travellers. The Chantry is believed to have been founded in 1296 by Richard of Morpeth.

The original bridge was only 11ft wide and this, with its humped design, made it dangerous for mail coaches with at least one, together with its passengers, ending up in the river. It was replaced by the present bridge, built in 1831 by Thomas Telford.

The various uses of the Chantry included that of a grammar school for boys.

After the Dissolution of the monasteries, the intention had also been to close chantries but Morpeth successfully petitioned to be allowed to continue with the school in the building. The school stayed put until 1846, with part of the building in use as a chapel.

When the school moved out, the Chantry was sold to private individuals and, at one time, housed a pop factory or, more formally, George Young's Aerated Waters Manufactory, established 1872.

In 1965, Morpeth Antiquarian Society opened a small local history museum in what had been the ladies' loos. Later, the Chantry was bought and restored by Castle Morpeth Council.

Pipe-playing and the convivial setting of a pub are a perfect match.

Indeed, Northumbrian pipers meet twice a month in a Morpeth hostelry.

And the town at one time had at least 30 pubs. They catered for the weekly livestock market, which in the 19th Century was said to be second only to London's Smithfield.

Drovers, farmers, butchers and buyers would have been a thirsty clientele and innkeepers also provided rough and ready beds and meals, and paddocks for the animals.

It was recorded that in 1832 over 200 oxen and 2,500 sheep and lambs sold weekly at Morpeth. In the year ending 1835, 20,000 cattle and 150,000 lambs, sheep, pigs and calves were sent south from the town.

Livestock pens filled the main town thoroughfares of Bridge and Newgate Streets, and old photographs give more than a whiff of the Wild West.

The market charter dates from 800 years ago but it was the 19th Century when livestock dealing truly took off. Drovers herded their charges from Scotland, the Borders, Northumberland and Cumbria. To make a Wednesday market, they left Scotland on a Friday.

There were five hostelries in a row in Bridge Street. The Queens Head, there since the 18th Century; Kings Head, demolished in the 1930s; Turks Head; the George and Dragon and Earl Grey which both closed in the 1970s. Beeswing House, in Newgate Street, is another former pub. It was named after a celebrated racehorse.

Entertainment in the late 18th Century included bull-baiting, with the unfortunate beast tied to a stone in the middle of the Market Place.

After a long journey to market and money having changed hands, the inclination would have been to make merry with ale and music.

Whether the pipers got in on the act depends on whether strict rules governing trade and the provision of services in the early 18th Century had been relaxed a century later.

In the early 1700s, musicians could not play in town without permission from Morpeth's official fiddler and piper. Transgressors faced a fine "or to have their pypes or instruments of musicke taken from them".

William Cocks, who died in 1971, was a master clockmaker from Ryton in Gateshead – and a member of the Newcastle Society of Antiquaries for 51 years.

He was, by all accounts, a shy man who devoted much of his time to making, playing and collecting bagpipes. A meticulous individual, he kept a record of every transaction he made and a maintenance log of each set of pipes he produced or purchased, and he backed it all up with research and the gathering of historical material on the bagpipes.

On his death, he left his collection to the Society of Antiquaries, which kept it in its base at the Black Gate in Newcastle for 15 years.

During that time, Northumbrian piper Colin Ross was honorary curator of the collection.

It was transferred to the Chantry where it would be more accessible to the public and where conditions were better for the instruments.

Colin is chairman of the Northumbrian Pipers Society, which is growing steadily and has over 700 members.

As well as playing, Colin makes sets of pipes. He says: "I have always felt

Belfries and churches are usually inseparable. But not so in Morpeth.

The town's Clock Tower, a scheduled ancient monument, is one of the few free-standing secular bell towers in England.

Morpeth is also unique in England in still ringing a nightly curfew bell, sponsored by the town council.

The sixth of the eight bells is the one delegated to sound the curfew, which was a signal to townspeople to wind down with the expectation of another hard day's graft to come.

Colin Wheeler, long-serving tower captain, says: "The Clock Tower is the heritage heart of Morpeth."

By an historical twist, it is the bells of Berwick which are heard in Morpeth.

The original six bells were cast in Berwick by Richard Phelps and incorporated a 1705 coin set in the metal of one.

The bells were intended as a gift to Berwick by Major General Edmond Maine in anticipation of his election as MP for the town.

But after Berwick rejected him, he took himself and his bells off to Morpeth, which did elect him.

An extra storey was built on to the tower to accommodate the bells, and a further two were added in 1833.

Because of wear and tear, the bells were melted down and re-cast to celebrate the Festival of Britain in 1951 – and the 1705 coin was included in the new casting. It is thought that the present Clock Tower was built using medieval stone from an earlier tower used to store valuables in the event of Scottish raids.

Previous uses of the Clock Tower have included a jail and a store for the town's hand-pulled fire engine.

There are around 20 bell ringers, and younger members who trained at Morpeth have gone on to be master ringers around the country.

that the pipes evoke the moors and hills, which make up a large part of the county. Scots abroad feel the same way about the Highland pipes and the same applies to people from the North-East.

"The Northumbrian pipes are very particular to Northumberland and North Durham and if we lost them then it would be like losing a language.

"They are something we can't afford to lose. You can open as many posh bars and restaurants as you like, but people are proud of their cultural heritage."

Bagpipes have been played in England for, it seems, at least 600 years. Another instrument, the Border or half-long bagpipes - bigger and better for playing outdoors - are also used in Northumberland and lowland Scotland. The Northumbrian small pipes operate by bellows pumped by the player's arm.

"It started out as a little instrument which played simple tunes," says Colin.

But that changed when keys were fitted which improved the small pipes' versatility and allowed the adaptation of fiddle music.

Famous pipe makers include Jamie Allan, born in Hepple in

Left: Northumbrian pipers at The Chantry

Above: Morpeth Castle

Northumberland in the 1730s. He appears to have been a bit of a lad. He was employed at Alnwick Castle but is said to have deserted from the Army and to have married three times. He died in 1810 in the Durham House of Correction after being sentenced to transportation following a conviction for horse stealing. But he still had his fans. A free pardon from the Prince Regent arrived just after Jamie's death.

The first piper to be employed by the Duke and Duchess of Northumberland was Joseph Turnbull, whose portrait of 1756 hangs in the castle.

John Dunn was making pipes in Newcastle in the late 18th and early 19th Centuries while Robert Reid, born in 1784 and based in North Shields, is held to be the finest maker of the small pipes. He was succeeded by his son, James.

Pipemakers in the 20th Century included Jack Armstrong and Bill Hedworth, from Gateshead.

Among today's pipe makers are David Burleigh, who first set up in business in Morpeth in the early 1970s and is now based in Longframlington.

Over the last 35 years, David has made 2,879 sets of Northumbrian small

Morpeth has been a town of two castles.

And architect John Dobson did his best to persuade people passing through that the figure should be three as he designed his Court House in the 1820s to look distinctly castle-like – battlements and all.

The 72ft high building was the gateway to the former octagonal Morpeth Prison and Dobson drew his inspiration for the Court House from the castles at Caernarvon, Conway and Beaumaris.

The first castle at Morpeth is believed to have been sited on Ha' Hill, which is now part of the town's Carlisle Park.

It is thought that there was a castle on the hill in 1095, built by William de Merley who had been granted the barony of Morpeth by William the Conqueror.

One of the occupational hazards for barons in the old days was backing the wrong side and when William died in 1087, de Merley supported Conqueror's son Robert Curthose – who built the first castle at Newcastle – for the throne against his brother William Rufus.

The de Merleys joined Robert de Mowbray, Earl of Northumberland, in this venture but, unfortunately for them, it was William Rufus who prevailed.

He came north to settle a few scores and is believed to have destroyed the Ha' Hill castle.

Eventually, a replacement castle was built. Stonework found in 1830 suggests that this castle had a stone keep in the 12th Century.

But trouble was never far away in those times and the de Merleys made a doubtful choice again when they joined other local notables in paying homage to the Scottish King Alexander II at Felton in Northumberland in 1215. The English King John was not amused and laid waste to Morpeth Castle.

By the early 15th Century, another castle had been built nearby and a survey in 1604 shows a keep with a gatehouse.

It met its day of reckoning during the English Civil War when General Leslie and his Scots marched into England to support the Parliamentarians at the Battle of Marston Moor.

He left a garrison of 500 at Morpeth Castle whose commander described his new quarters as "this ruinous hole". Ruinous or not, it took the 2,700-strong Royalist regiment of the Marquis of Montrose, with six cannon, 20 days to take the castle.

In the 19th Century the castle gatehouse was restored for the Earl of Carlisle.

It was the Countess of Carlisle who gave to the town the land which was to become Carlisle Park in 1928.

Just after the Second World War, the gatehouse was bought by the local authority and was rented out as the country's most unusual council house.

But by the 1980s extensive repairs were needed and in 1988 the gatehouse was leased by the Landmark Trust, a charity which specialises in rescuing unusual historic buildings and letting them for holidays.

The restoration of the gatehouse was completed in 1991 and it now offers accommodation for up to seven holidaymakers.

The 1820s prison behind the Court House block replaced the old gaol in Bridge Street, which is now a council one-stop shop.

Dobson's prison incorporated debtors' and felons' sections, a treadmill and governor's house all surrounded by 20ft high walls.

The prison was demolished in 1891. The Court House remained and is now mostly apartments, no doubt of a superior specification than what was afforded to the original occupants of the site.

pipes, supplying anywhere from the Falkland Islands to Nepal and Alaska.

The Northumbrian pipes have been brought to a wider audience by local players like Kathryn Tickell and Pauline Cato.

Colin Ross, who has played the Northumbrian pipes for 40 years, says: "I have always been fascinated by the pipes. Bagpipes developed in medieval times and, compared to other instruments of the time, they were the electrical instruments of their day. They were extraordinarily powerful. "

The Chantry can be contacted on (01670) 500-700.

Anthony Spires dressed as William Turner

Morpeth's Famous Names

When Morpeth's Carlisle Park was given a £2m makeover,
courtesy of the Heritage Lottery Fund, the chance was taken to pay
suitable tribute to one of the town's most illustrious sons.

A garden was created to commemorate William Turner, born in Morpeth around 1508 and whose father was a tanner.

Turner, who is believed to have attended the school in Morpeth's Chantry, went on to become one of the influential figures of the 16th Century.

He is accorded the title of the father of English botany, and was also an outstanding natural scientist, ornithologist, physician and churchman.

The Carlisle Park garden, with many plants which Turner would recognise, opened in 2002.

Two years later Turner was once more on the national stage when Castle Morpeth Council exhibited a version of the garden at the Chelsea Flower Show.

Visitors could enjoy aspects of the garden such as six physic beds containing herbs and themed according to what the plants were used to treat, such as wounds and broken bones; heart, lungs and blood; bites, stings and poisons; digestion, stomach and liver; depression and dreams; head, hair, eyes and teeth.

But few would have known how eventful a life Turner lived.

In 1526 he went to Pembroke Hall,

At the 14th Century St Mary's Church in Morpeth is the grave of suffragette Emily Davison, who died after running in front of the King's horse Anmer at the Derby on June 4, 1913.

Emily was born in London in 1872 but was raised at Longhorsley, near Morpeth. After a university education, she worked as a teacher but gave up the job as she became increasingly involved in the Women's Social and Political Union.

In the fight for the vote for women, she spent several spells in prison for obstruction, stone-throwing and setting fire to post boxes. While on hunger strike, she was force-fed.

She described the experience in a letter to a friend: "In the evening the matron, two doctors, and five or six wardresses entered the cell. The scene which followed will haunt me with its horror all my life, and is almost indescribable. While they held me flat, the elder doctor tried all round my mouth with a steel gag to find an opening.

"On the right side of my mouth two teeth are missing; this gap he found, pushed in the horrid instrument, and prised open my mouth to its widest extent. Then a wardress poured liquid down my throat out of a tin enamelled cup. What it was I cannot say, but there was some medicament, which was foul to the last degree.

"As I would not swallow the stuff and jerked it out with my tongue, the doctor pinched my nose and somehow gripped my tongue with the gag. The torture was barbaric."

On one occasion she barricaded her cell, which was filled with water from a hose trained into the space by wardens. This affected her health and later in court she was awarded damages of 40 shillings.

It is not clear whether the Derby tragedy was a protest which went wrong or a deliberate act by Emily.

Suffragette Christobel Pankhurst wrote: "Emily Davison paid with her life for making the whole world understand that women were in earnest for the vote. Probably in no other way and at no other time and place could she so effectively have brought the concentrated attention of millions to bear upon the cause."

Crowds turned out for Emily's funeral procession in London and for the journey of her coffin from Morpeth railway station to St Mary's Church.

One of the North's great heroes, the Newcastle-born Admiral Lord Collingwood, spent 44 years, on and off, at sea.

In 1761, at just 12 years of age, he joined the navy and sailed off on the 28-gun frigate Shannon to begin a career which reached a pinnacle at the Battle of Trafalgar, where he played a crucial part.

On one of his longest spells ashore, he met Sarah Blackett, of Charlotte Square in Newcastle, who was the daughter of Mayor John Blackett.

In 1791 they were married in St Nicholas Cathedral and set up home at a rented house in Oldgate in Morpeth, which they later bought.

They had two daughters in two years, Sarah and Mary Patience, and it is at Morpeth that we catch a glimpse of the other Collingwood: busy in his garden, family and town life and walking the countryside planting acorns from his pocket to provide the oak for future ships.

In 1802 he was back in Morpeth and writing to his sister-in-law in the South: "I would recommend Northumberland for your residence. It has fine healthy air. The bathing at Newbiggin has given Sarah health and strength."

Collingwood bought adjoining plots around his house to open up views down to the River Wansbeck.

A fellow admiral, calling at the house, found Collingwood and his gardener, Mr Scott, at the bottom of a trench they were digging.

Max Adams, author of the book Collingwood: Northumberland's Heart of Oak, says: "Collingwood seems to have known everyone in Morpeth.

"He was devoted to his house, wife and daughters. But he also probably had the sailor's disease of when at sea always thinking of Morpeth, and

Left: Collingwood House, Morpeth

Centre: Lord Collingwood

Above: Entrance to Collingwood House

when in Morpeth thinking of the sea. I think he found it a difficult act to juggle, especially missing so much of the upbringing of his daughters.

"If he had not been born into an era of naval warfare, he may well have ended up as the headmaster of a school and been perfectly happy."

The house at Side in Newcastle, where Collingwood was born, is gone but his home in Morpeth remains as a kind of monument.

Cambridge, to study and embraced Protestantism at a time when firmly-held religious beliefs could be a matter of life and death, depending who was on the throne. Turner became senior treasurer of his college and produced his first work on herbs.

But the dangerous mix of religion and politics forced the newly-married Turner into exile in Europe, where he ended up qualifying in medicine in Italy.

Returning to England as physician to the Duke of Somerset, he published his *Names of Herbs* in 1548 and then, in 1551, the first of what would be a great three-part work – his *Herbal*.

Turner described around 300 plants in the *Herbal*, illustrated by woodcuts, in scientific detail and in what was the first botanical study to be written in English so that the knowledge was made widely available.

There are references to locations of plants growing around Morpeth and the "Wanspeke".

In the *Herbal* he also described the "uses and vertues" of the plants.

Of parsley, he wrote: "The seed taken beforehand helpeth men that have weak brains to bear drink better."

Turner became Dean of Wells Cathedral, and his puritan side comes to the fore in his comments on cowslips, where he deplored the fact that "some women sprinkle the flowers of the Cowslip with white wine and wash their faces ... to drive wrinkles away, and to make them fair in the eyes of the world rather than in the eyes of God".

He adopted the same attitude over marigolds which "some use to make their hair yellow, not being content with the natural colour which God hath given them".

Turner also wrote the first printed book devoted entirely to birds, and the first to treat them in a modern scientific spirit.

His writings on fish include references to a type of cod caught at Beadnell, Northumberland.

After Mary Tudor came to the throne, it was exile again for Turner, this time in Germany.

Back once more in England, he published the complete edition of his *Herbal* in 1568, the year he died. Morpeth's Chantry has a first edition of the *Herbal*, signed by its original 16th Century owner William Pickering, who was ambassador to France.

The book was bequeathed to Morpeth Mechanics

In 1782 in Bullers Green, Morpeth, Robert Morrison was born, a boy destined to be the first Protestant missionary to China.

His family later moved to Newcastle and lived near Cloth Market, where a paving stone marks the spot.

Robert decided to become a missionary in 1804, following the death of his mother.

He studied with the London Missionary Society, and volunteered to go to China.

Having learned to read and write Chinese, with the help of a Chinese student who he met in London, he sailed to Canton, via New York, in 1807.

While living in China, he mastered both Cantonese and Mandarin.

He married Mary Morton, daughter of an East India Company surgeon, in Macau and, in 1809, became translator to the East India Company's factory in Canton, securing a legal basis for residence and a means of supporting himself.

Morrison was a voluminous writer in both English and Chinese.

From 1814-19 he translated The Bible into Chinese and his Dictionary of the Chinese Language (1815-23), was published in 21 volumes.

Morrison returned to England only once in 27 years and preached to a packed congregation in the Presbyterian chapel in High Bridge, Newcastle.

While in England he remarried, his first wife having died in 1822.

He was appointed Chinese Secretary and Interpreter to Lord Napier, Superintendent for Trade with China in 1834, but died shortly after taking up the post and is buried in the Old Protestant Cemetery in Macao.

His son from his first marriage, John Robert Morrison, became secretary to the Hong Kong government.

Institute by the Earl of Carlisle.

Anthony Spires, Castle Morpeth Council parks and countryside manager, has an affinity with Turner.

He works from an ex-potting shed office in Carlisle Park next to the Turner garden and also dresses up as the 16th Century botanist from time to time – most notably at Chelsea.

He says: "Turner was an absolutely brilliant man. For the *Herbal*, he wrote not in Latin but in English and explained the uses of plants for the common man. He was a man of the people.

"It is amazing how things have come full-circle and how many people now are interested in herbal medicine."

Carlisle Park, opened in 1929, is a showpiece for Morpeth.

But the town also has what is claimed to be the smallest registered park in the country.

Mafeking Park was once a reasonable size but that changed when major roads were re-routed.

Now Mafeking Park is confined to a roundabout opposite Morpeth Cenotaph and consists of a lime tree, heathers and 20 annual bedding plants.

Bolam

Around 100,000 people a year beat a path to Bolam Lake Country Park in Northumberland.

Bolam Lake

It is a prime day-out destination, with visitors enjoying its 100 acres of open space, woodland and grassland paths, and its 25-acre lake and reedbeds which provide important wildlife habitats.

But while today Bolam is all about leisure, its creation was the result of a much more serious state of affairs.

Local landowner Lord Decies felt compelled to do something for the locals at a time of agricultural and economic slump.

His answer was to fashion Bolam Lake and woodlands from what was a naturally boggy area.

Northumberland historian John Hodgson wrote how Lord Decies "who to give employment to the poor, in the scarce and disastrous winters of 1816 and 1817, converted the splashy lands of Bolam bog into a fair expanse of water, and has covered the rough and ferny hillsides with plantations".

The workers earned a shilling a day for their labours and only returned the next day if they so wished.

It was Newcastle architect John Dobson who in 1816 began the design of the Bolam Lake landscape before he went to work on a batch of mansions in the area in future years.

St Andrew's Church, Bolam

Willy Schludecker

Few of the many visitors to Bolam Lake will make the short hop around the corner to St Andrew's Church.

And they are missing something very special.

The church, where people have worshipped for more than 1,000 years, is one of the most tranquil and attractive in Northumberland. Apart from a neighbouring former rectory, the church now stands alone following the disappearance of the original Bolam village it served.

But the old gravestones in the churchyard tell the community's story, against a backdrop view of the outline of Simonside on the skyline.

The oldest part of the church is its Anglo-Saxon tower. The decorative door dates from about 1200 and inside there is a Norman arch and late 12th Century columns. It looks

much as it would have looked in the 14th Century. It contains the effigy of Robert Raymes, of Aydon and Shortflatt, who died in 1323.

The private house at Shortflatt, a mile from the church, includes the tower which Reymes was given permission to fortify in 1305.

Lord Decies, who created Bolam Lake, erected a stone memorial in the church grounds in memory of John and Margaret Charlton, "for upwards of 60 years the faithful and respected servants of the Bolam family". But all this history could have been obliterated during Wold War 2.

On May 1, 1942, German pilot Willy Schludecker's Dornier 217 bomber was intercepted by RAF fighters. In his bid to escape, he jettisoned his four 500kg bombs over the Northumberland countryside.

One exploded near the vicarage, and another two in fields.

The fourth smashed through the church wall but didn't detonate. The hole was converted into a stained glass window, with a message: "This window marks the place where on 1st May 1942 a bomb dropped by a German aircraft entered the church but did not explode." A graphic, first-hand account of the incident is given in a letter to the Vicar of Bolam's son, Flying Officer John Hutton, who was based in the Middle East. It was written by his mother and reads: "We are safe and well and not duly alarmed after Jerry paid us a visit at 4am on May 1st. He was being hotly pursued by two of our fighters.

"He was very low down and discharged the whole of his load in order to get away. Four

Bomb Window at Bolam

bombs, one fell just missing the walnut tree. An unexploded one lay in the chancel. It had passed through tower part of the wall in the H. D. Chapel, smashing all the furnishings in that part, injuring some windows.

"Providence watched over us that morning, for our house still stands. Windows and lots of frames gone. Roof badly damaged, doors broken or damaged, glass everywhere.

"We were smothered with it in bed and not even a scratch. The remaining two bombs only made large craters in Windmill field. People have been most kind. We had breakfast with the Allendales. They had only three broken windows and a bit of ceiling down."

At the age of 82, Willy travelled from his home near Cologne to the church after hearing what had happened from air war historian Bill Norman.

He met people who had experienced it and apologised for the damage.

Willy noted that locals were "friendly and forgiving" and that one of the craters caused by one of his bombs was now an attractive pond. Willy's war included 120 flights, nine crash landings and the Iron Cross.

Dobson, who had a strong interest in landscape gardening, was commissioned by Lord Decies to lay out the artificial lake, the dam at its eastern end, "necessary islands" and adjacent woodland plantations.

No doubt most of the workforce came from the old – but now vanished – settlement of Bolam. It lay between Bolam Hall, which still stands today, and St Andrew's Church.

Edward I granted Bolam a market and fair in 1305. At that time the community included a castle, and the church, and was said to have had 200 houses.

There are reports that the village was raided and put to the torch in the 16th Century and, during work on Bolam Hall, fire-damaged stonework was revealed.

But the Bolam area has an exceedingly long history of settlement.

A two-and-a-half mile circular walk from Bolam Lake skirts Slate Hill, from which slate was quarried for roofing material. But it was originally an Iron Age fortified settlement.

The walk also passes near Huckhoe Settlement, another Iron Age site which was used intermittently for the next 1,200 years.

Archaeologist John Davies, from Stannington, has been investigating the Bolam area for the last 20 years. He was part of a dig on a sandstone ridge near Bolam Lake, which revealed evidence of how Northumberland's first Neolithic farmers lived around 6,000 years ago.

"There was a tremendous amount going on around here," says John.

It was the first early Neolithic site to be discovered in southern Northumberland and it was investigated after field

walking by John turned up flint and pottery evidence.

One of the star finds was a stone axe from the Langdale 'axe factory' in the Lake District, which may have been exchanged for prestige goods such as pottery.

The axe, which had been broken by use, was found in one of a number of rubbish dumps together with flints, charred hazelnut shells – hazelnuts were a favourite snack – and pottery.

The thick, broad-bottomed pots would have acted like woks when placed on the hearth and would have spread the heat quickly and easily.

The excavation revealed a number of hearth pits which would have contained embers or hot stones and game would have been thrown in and covered up to bake.

At nearby Shortflatt Barrows is an untouched Bronze Age mound. Back in recent times, Land Army girls worked during the Second World War on felling timber at Bolam Lake for pay of 12 shillings a week.

Italian prisoners of war were also employed in timber-cutting operations, which were served by a light railway.

After the war, the estate deteriorated and in 1972 Northumberland County Council bought the lake and some of the woodland, creating the country park.

Bolam Lake has a visitor centre and shop. Telephone (01661) 881-234.

It is a three-mile circular walk from Bolam Lake to the village of Harnham – and the tragic tale of 17th Century celebrated beauty Katherine Babington.

Katherine was the wife of Major Philip Babington, a Cromwellian officer who had been governor of Berwick Castle.

Both puritans, they moved to the manor house and tower at Harnham. It became a centre for puritan sympathisers and non conformists as Charles II and the Church of England returned.

Katherine was so attractive that magistrates at Durham issued an order obliging her to eat in back rooms of establishments in the city: if she was in front rooms crowds gathered and blocked the roads.

But Katherine could be as bullish as she was beautiful and in 1646 she had the Rev Forster, who had returned to his living at Bolam Church, pulled from the pulpit.

She was prosecuted for contempt and avoided going to prison on condition that she be held captive in a room in her husband's tower.

This was her life until she died in 1670. Permission for her burial in consecrated ground was refused. Her coffin was placed in a vault hacked out of the rock below the tower, with a plaque which reads:

"My time is past, as you may see
I viewed the dead as you do me
Or long you' ll lie as low as I
And some will look on thee."

The religious thread at Harnham remains as it is the site of a Buddhist monastery known as Ratanagiri, which means 'jewel on the hill'.

Thirlwall Castle

The Roman legacy so dominates the central sector of Hadrian's Wall country in Northumberland that it is easy to overlook the centuries of history which followed the legions.

A reminder is the castle which stands in a gap in the line of the wall – a feature which gave the fortification its name: Thirl-Wall.

Thirlwall Castle was built in the 1330s above the wooded banks of the Tipalt Burn, which is now a site of special scientific interest, near Greenhead. The burn can be vigorous in full spate and would have washed away whatever arrangements the Romans made to carry the wall over the gap.

The four-storey castle, with turrets and tower, doubled as a defended home in the years of Anglo-Scottish conflict and as a symbol of the status of the Thirlwall family.

There was, no doubt, a touch of rivalry with families like the Blenkinsopps, who were building nearby Blenkinsopp Castle.

Thirlwall Castle was nothing if not solidly built and sheltered the family for 300 years.

The castle is a key feature in Northumberland National Park. It is one of only eight Grade I listed buildings in the park and is also a scheduled ancient monument, as well as being an example of how medieval life was lived in what was a remote area.

It combines two of Northumberland's most important historical periods – the Roman occupation and the time of the Border wars.

"There is so much emphasis on the Roman remains but Thirlwall

Castle tells us a different story," says the national park's Albert Weir, who led a project to preserve the building.

"There is a big gap about which we know little between the Romans leaving and the first visits by 18th Century antiquarians to the area.

"Thirlwall is one of the few medieval buildings along the Wall and one of the few pieces of evidence of early medieval life."

The castle - or, more strictly, fortified hall house - replaced an earlier dwelling which was good enough to accommodate

Edward I in 1306.

The Thirlwalls had done well out of military service in the wars of the 14th Century, serving with Edward III, the Black Prince, and the Duke of Lancaster in France and with Richard II in Scotland.

But no matter how adept the family was militarily, they still needed a secure base in what were troubled times.

John Thirlwall chose the spot at the Tipalt Burn, which was surrounded by hill top positions from which raiders could be spotted and all the

Black Middens bastle

Not far from Thirlwall Castle, on a tributary of the Tipalt Burn, is Low Old Shield, a bastle which has been converted into a farmhouse.

Places like Thirlwall Castle were built by the landowners. But it was the tenant farmers who constructed the bastles, or defendable farmhouses, at the start of the 17th Century.

Almost three centuries of wars with Scotland were followed by the Reiver years of raiding by clans such as the Halls, Hedleys, Charltons, Dodds, Milburns, Robsons, Armstrongs, Nixons, Scotts and Elliots.

After the Union of the Crowns in 1603, the feuding and thieving persisted in an area which was far from central Government and where the terrain and the expense made it difficult to impose the rule of law. It engendered many decades of lawlessness and sparked a surge of bastle-building in the early years of the 1600s.

The remains of around 50 bastles survive in Northumberland National Park and 200 in the county overall.

They were sometimes built in clusters, as at Tarset near Bellingham and the village of Wall near Hexham.

Bastles had stout stone walls and a basement where livestock could be locked away at times of attack, with the family retreating to the upper storey – pulling up the ladder after them – where the windows were small and barred.

Some bastles had quenching holes for use if raiders built a fire against the ground floor wooden door. Water would be poured out of the hole to put out the fire.

In later years when times became more peaceful, external stone stairs were built on to some bastles.

Good examples of bastles which can be visited include Black Middens at Tarset, which is under the guardianship of English Heritage.

Bastles survive as ruins and were also expanded into more comfortable farmhouses. Some, like Black Middens, were used as farm outbuildings.

Northumberland-based buildings archaeologist Peter Ryder has carried out a study on Northumberland.

"People build bastles to protect themselves from those in the next valley," he says.

"Bastles were a deterrent. Raiders wanted to catch you in the open and didn't want to spend time besieging a place.

"Bastles are a reflection of a troubled past and a lawless zone, and a unique time in border life.

"While castles, towers and defended manor houses were built by the landowners, bastles are the earliest surviving buildings which were constructed by ordinary folk."

Before being given the protection worthy of a world heritage site, Hadrian's Wall was subject to varying degrees of exploitation.

Stone was used to build farmhouses and fortresses such as Thirlwall Castle.

Chunks of the wall also disappeared in a century of quarrying for the hard whinstone which was used mainly for road building.

At Walltown Quarry near Thirlwall, the wheel turned full circle and a crater left by blasting and digging has turned into another attraction in Northumberland National Park.

In the 1870s, the Northumberland Whinstone Company quarried at Walltown. The crags carrying the wall were blown apart. But in a restoration programme, clay excavated during the building of Greenhead bypass was used to soften the quarry contours.

In 1985, Walltown was taken over by the National Park and now there are ponds, trails, toilets and a picnic site. Visitors can follow the hard rock quarry trail and spot fossils in stretches of exposed sandstone.

In the Whin Sill crag face they can see the joints that formed as the dolerite rock cooled. The joints cause rock to break into columns with the best examples at the Giant's Causeway in Northern Ireland and Fingal's Cave on the Scottish island of Staffa. Small holes in the dolerite at Walltown are where gas bubbles were trapped when the rock was molten.

Lesley Silvera, who helped set up the trail, says: "Walltown is now like a robust country park which has been geared up for visitor use and it is an attractive place for families."

The Pennine Way and Hadrian's Wall trail also pass through Walltown. A four-tonne block of whinstone, airlifted out of the quarry, was sent to Holland and is now part of an international monument to children.

Off the track along the quarry is woodland with a spectacular display of bluebells in the springtime.

materials he needed were at hand – timber, water, lime, and thousands of dressed Roman stones.

The castle had a Great Hall, servants' quarters, ground floor stabling for the horses when attacks came, and a dungeon in the base of a turret.

Defensive though it was, the castle was also a home. There is a glimpse of domesticity in Lancelot Thirlwall's will in 1582 in which he left property to his wife and eight children including "fetherbedes, pillowes, brasse pottes, candlesticks, table napkins. a long spit and hyves of bees."

The beginning of the end for Thirlwall came when, in the early 16th Century, Lancelot Thirlwall married Janet Errington, who brought with her an estate at Newbiggin, near Hexham.

The lake at Walltown

River at Greenhead

It was Newbiggin in the Tyne Valley, rather than Thirlwall in the uplands, which became the favoured family residence.

Thirlwall was occupied by Scottish forces on behalf of Parliament during the English Civil War and by 1723 the castle was classed as a rented "tenement".

In 1748 it was sold for £4,000 to the Earl of Carlisle, who was more interested in the land and allowed the building to decay, its descent into ruins attracted the attention of artists and historians.

The east wall fell into the Tipalt Burn in 1831 and falls of masonry were still happening in the 1980s.

In 1999, the National Park acquired a 99-year lease on the castle and 25 acres of adjacent woodland. The park was successful in winning almost £500,000

from the Heritage Lottery Fund and European Union to preserve the castle. Up went scaffolding and experts carried out surveys involving an endoscope – an instrument with a camera attached – to look deep into spaces within the structure to identify and safeguard the roosting places of pipistrelle and natterjack bats and the nesting sites for birds like swifts.

There was also the opportunity to record the rare lichens living on top of the ruins. Grasses and flowers, such as ivy-leaved toad flax, were removed and kept alive during the restoration of the stonework, then returned to the walls.

Lime mortar was used in the conservation work, as cement is hostile to lichens. And 1,250 native trees were also planted near the castle.

It was the first time in the North-East that the restoration of a historic building had involved keeping plants and returning them when the job was done.

"It was quite a pioneering venture. It was like working on a historic tapestry – we wanted it to be the case that people could not see that we had intervened," says Albert.

The castle is now open to the public for the first time in 600 years and, being at the junction of the Pennine Way and the Hadrian's Wall national trails, it now has more admirers than ever.

Black Middens bastle can be reached off the A68, via the B6320 through Greenhaugh.

There is a car park and a Reiver's Trail of either two-and-a-half miles or four miles, following the Tarset Burn and taking in several bastles.

Thirlwall Castle is reached via the A69 to Greenhead or B6318. There are three walks: two strolls from the castle car park or Greenhead, and a half-mile walk from Walltown Quarry, signposted off the B6318.

Next to Walltown, the Roman Army Museum is open mid-February to March, 10am-5pm, April to September. Call 01697 747 485.